Homemade
Christmas

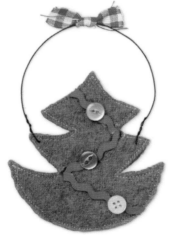

Homemade Christmas

Create your own gifts, cards,
decorations, and recipes

LONDON, NEW YORK,
MELBOURNE, MUNICH, DELHI

Designer Vanessa Hamilton
Project Editor Elizabeth Yeates
Illustrator Vanessa Hamilton
Pre-Production Producer Rebecca Fallowfield
Senior Producer Katherine Whyte
Special Sales Creative Project Manager
Alison Donovan

First published in the United States in 2014
by DK Publishing
345 Hudson Street, New York, New York 10014

Material previously published as:
A Greener Christmas (2008), Soup (2009),
Fresh Flower Arranging (2011), Craft (2012),
Hors d'Oeuvres (2012), Family Cookbook (2013),
Handmade Gifts (2013), Step-by-Step Cake
Decorating (2013), and Vegetables Please (2013)

Copyright © 2008, 2009, 2011, 2012, 2013, 2014
Dorling Kindersley Limited

2 4 6 8 10 9 7 5 3 1

001 – 274591 – Aug/14

A catalog record for this book is available
from the Library of Congress

ISBN 978-1-4654-3259-9

Printed and bound in China by
Hung Hing Printing Co. Ltd

Discover more at
www.dk.com

Contents

Personal Gifts

Dinner and Dessert

Introduction

For many people, Christmas is their favorite time of year: decorating the home and tree, wrapping and sending presents, and bringing together friends and family. This year, create a truly unique and crafty Christmas by making your own gorgeous gifts and decorations, and planning a wondeful Christmas feast complete with trimmings and amazing desserts.

Every idea in *Homemade Christmas* is explained in step-by-step detail so you get professional-looking results. There are lots of ideas for how you can add your own twist, so you can make this Christmas perfectly yours. Get into the Christmas spirit and begin!

1

Home
Decoration

Make a dried leaf wreath

Dressing your front door with a wreath at Christmas time helps to create a wonderfully warm, festive welcome to your home. The only downside is that you can't enjoy the wreath indoors. The solution is to hang another, more delicate, decorative wreath in your living room or hallway: collect fallen leaves and seed heads in the fall and turn them into this stunning arrangement.

Materials

- Richly colored leaves
- Sheets of newspaper
- 1 large circular wire wreath frame, available from florists or mail-order companies
- Thin wire
- Mesh ribbon
- Eco-friendly adhesive glue

Craft tip

Collecting leaves

Look for fallen leaves in early and mid-fall before the weather takes its toll. Red oak (Quercus rubra) and maple (Acer) are good choices. Depending on the room temperature and type of leaf, they can take up to a week to dry out and flatten.

1 Arrange leaves in a single layer between sheets of newspaper under a mat or piece of carpet, or place a couple of heavy books on top.

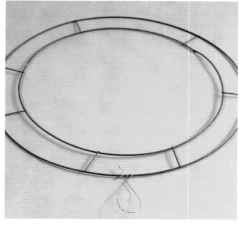

2 Once the flattened leaves are completely dry, make up the wreath. Secure the wire in a loop and attach it to the top of the frame.

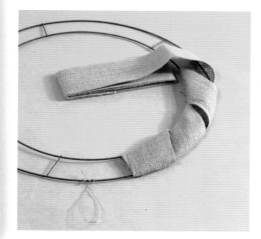

3 Wrap the mesh ribbon around the frame in a zig-zag fashion. Staple it onto the frame at intervals to cover the frame completely.

4 Glue large leaves onto the mesh, stems pointing inward, so that they overlap slightly. Glue small leaves on top in an even pattern. Allow to dry.

Fabric garland

This charming garland is versatile enough to decorate mantlepieces, kitchen dressers, Christmas trees, and bedrooms. Store it carefully and it can be reused every year. You can make your own felt by washing an old, unwanted, cream-colored 100 percent wool blanket or garment in a hot machine wash.

Materials

- Garland templates (pp.270–73)
- Large piece of cream-colored felt
- Brown felt for the gingerbread man
- Scissors
- Pins
- Eco-friendly marker pen
- Colored embroidery thread (for blanket stitching and features) and needle
- Ricrac trimming
- 5 lengths of wire, each about 3 in (8 cm) long
- 3 ft (1 m) twine or string
- Pieces of recycled ribbon
- Old, unwanted woollen garment or scarf
- Recycled buttons

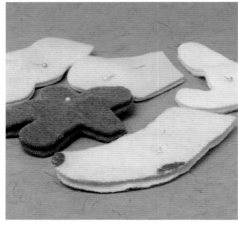

1 Cut and pin together two of each shape from cream felt, and two gingerbread men from brown felt. Decorate one stocking with the pen.

2 Sew the shapes together. Leave the mitten and stocking tops unsewn. Sew on the features and ricrac trimming (see pp.18–19).

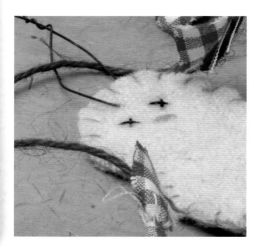

3 Thread a piece of wire through the top of each shape and secure in a loop. Thread the twine through the loops and tie ribbons onto the twine.

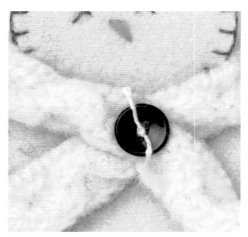

4 Cut strips from the garment for scarves and sew them, together with some decorative ribbons and buttons, onto the fabric shapes.

Fabric garland variations

Mitten Sew a folded length of recycled ribbon and a vintage button on to the front of the mitten. Leave the top unstitched.

Robin Cut a circle of fabric (p.273), fold in half, insert a fabric beak, and sew the curved edges together. Add wings and a red breast.

Christmas tree Cut two tree shapes (p.272) from green felt, sew them together, and decorate with ricrac trimming and buttons.

Snowman Sew two eyes and draw a carrot nose with a fabric pen, then attach a length of wool fabric as a scarf with a button.

Stocking Embroider simple details on to the toe and heel of the sock. Decorate with a folded length of ribbon and a button.

Gingerbread man Sew ricrac trimming on to the arms and feet, and cut out and sew on a scarf and button in jolly colors.

Holly and berries Cut two holly shapes (p.281) from plaid fabric, sew them together, insert a wire circle, and add red berry buttons.

Candy cane Wrap a small length of brightly colored ribbon around the stick and secure it in place with a sewn-on button.

Christmas stocking

Stockings are a great way of giving gifts without having to wrap each item. They are also useful for decorating the home; if you hang them up early, they will add to the excitement of Christmas approaching. You can customize each stocking by sewing on a decorative bow, an individual's initials, or fabric shapes on a favorite theme, or wind a piece of trailing ivy around the top of the stocking.

Materials

- Embroidered tablecloth or an unwanted curtain
- Template (p274)
- Scissors
- Extra fabric to decorate
- Cotton thread and needle, or a sewing machine
- A piece of fabric 1 x 5 in (2.5 x 12 cm) for the loop

Green tip

Using recycled fabric

If someone has a much-loved garment that is no longer fit to wear, use it as the fabric for their stocking. If the material is very worn, sew it onto a piece of plain cotton or burlap material first, and then cut out the stocking shape.

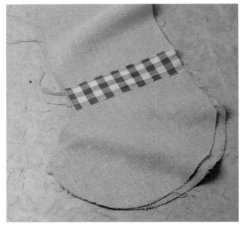

1 Cut out two stocking shapes using the template. Sew on any fabric details, such as a length of fabric, around the width of the stocking.

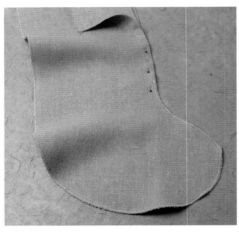

2 Align the shapes, correct sides facing inward, and sew together, leaving a seam of ½ in (1.5 cm) around the edge. Leave the top unstitched.

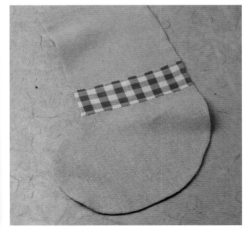

3 Fold over and sew the fabric at the top of the stocking so the edges don't show. Then turn the stocking the right way round.

4 Fold the fabric into a loop and sew it to the top of the stocking. Sew on more decorations as you wish. Make more stockings in the same way.

Scent a room

Delicately scented rooms are somehow more inviting, and the subtly uplifting aroma of a potpourri will make your home seem cosier. Collect a mixture of natural materials and aromatic spices, arrange them in your favorite bowl, and sprinkle over scented oils: the potpourri will look and smell lovely.

Potpourri recipes

Spice potpourri
Collect a few cinnamon sticks, star anise, a nutmeg or two, some cloves, and a selection of dried natural materials or some walnuts and hazelnuts. Sprinkle over 10 drops of cinnamon oil and 5 drops of clove oil.

Citrus potpourri
Dry some whole clementines, kumquats, orange and lemon slices, and orange and lemon peel. Sprinkle over 10 drops of orange oil and 5 drops of lemon oil.

Pine potpourri
Collect the cones and a few small branches of any fragrant evergreens—pine, juniper, Cyprus, and so on. Sprinkle over 10 drops of pine oil and 5 drops of cedar oil.

Garden potpourri
Gather a selection of natural materials such as thistles, berries, rosehips, and lavender and rosemary stems, and allow them to dry out throughly. Sprinkle over 10 drops of lavender oil and 5 drops of rosemary oil.

Potpourri is made of three ingredients: dried natural materials, which comprise the filling, and spices and scented oils to create fragrance. The natural materials can include whatever you find visually pleasing and suit the type of potpourri you're making. Collect interesting seasonal flowers, seed heads, flower heads, fruits, sprigs of foliage, and berries. To dry these ingredients thoroughly, spread them in a single layer on newspaper and leave for a week or so in a warm, dry place out of the sun and away from drafts. Fruits like oranges, lemons, and kumquats need to be dried slightly differently: cover a wire rack with cheesecloth, place the whole fruits or fruit slices in a single layer on top and leave in the oven on a low temperature or in a cabinet for up to 48 hours.

Making up a potpourri

Arrange the dried natural materials and spices in a large bowl and sprinkle a few drops of scented essential oil over them. Cover the potpourri in the bowl until needed and refresh with a few more drops of oil when necessary. Try mixing your own combination of scented oils to create a pleasing aroma, or follow a recipe (left).

Scenting a room quickly

Other, quicker ways of creating scent include placing pine cones, orange peel, or seasoned apple wood on top of a wood fire as it burns, and placing a saucer of orange peel or lemon peel, or small bowls of water containing a few drops of scented oil, next to a warm radiator.

Nature crafts techniques

Working with natural foliage provides the perfect excuse to go for a walk in your local park, woodland, or forest—or you may even find suitable greenery in your garden. Look out for items that have fallen off trees, such as pinecones and acorns. Using fresh cuttings of berries and firs creates a lovely seasonal aroma, or you can enhance the natural fragrance with a few drops of an appropriate fragrance oil.

Making a wreath frame

1 Strip two equal lengths of vine of their leaves. Secure them together by binding with a short length of fine wire.

2 Twist the vines together to make one strong length. Secure the other end with wire.

3 Bring the two ends together to create a circle. Twist the ends around each other and tie them together with a short length of wire. If the vines are too long, overlap the ends; if they're too short, introduce an additional length.

4 To strengthen the frame, add more lengths of stripped vine. Tie one end to the frame with wire and wind the vine around the frame, securing the other end with wire. Repeat until you have a strong, firm frame.

5 To keep the shape even and strengthen the frame more, tie small pieces of wire at regular intervals around the frame.

Working with fresh foliage

1 Ensure each stem of foliage is fresh, clean, and dry, and that it looks healthy. Avoid using materials that are moldy, as the mold may spread.

2 Use a sharp pair of scissors to trim foliage to the required size. For thick stems, use a pair of pruning shears. These speciality gardening scissors can cut through branches up to ¾ in (2 cm) thick.

Making fir bunches

Use a sharp pair of scissors to trim the sprigs of fir to 1½ in (4 cm) lengths. Take small bunches of fir (about five sprigs) and wind a length of wire around the bottom of their stems to hold them together.

Securing foliage to the frame

1 To secure fresh foliage such as fir bunches to the frame, use a short length of wire to wrap the base of the bunch to the frame.

2 Use superglue to attach dried foliage, cones, and other material. Apply a dot of glue to the base of the item and then press in place, making sure not to glue any other foliage together.

Keeping foliage fresh

Fresh foliage should last throughout the winter season, though it will wilt more quickly if it is left outdoors without shelter from the wind. Spritz it regularly with a fine mist of water to keep it fresh.

Enhancing the fragrance

Add a few drops of fragrance oil to fresh or dried foliage to enhance the natural fragrance.

Winter wreath

Wreaths are a great introduction to floristry, giving you a chance to work with both fresh and dried foliage. Here, bunches of fir create the base for the frame, and pine cones, acorns, and colorful berries are dotted around to add texture and color. You could also add leaves, dried fruits, and nuts to create a design that is unique and smells gorgeous.

Materials

- stripped vine stems
- selection of fresh foliage (fir sprigs, myrtle, berries, eucalyptus leaves)
- measuring tape
- selection of dried foliage (pinecones, acorns)
- fragrance oil (optional)

Equipment

- scissors or garden shears
- fine wire
- superglue
- hook or ribbon
- spray bottle

1 Follow making a wreath frame on p.24 to make a 12 in (30 cm) diameter circular frame. Around six rounds of vine will make a thick, sturdy frame.

2 Follow making fir bunches on p.25 to make 15–20 bunches. Attach each one to the frame with wire so that they face the same direction. Overlap one bunch with the next to cover the entire frame.

3 Trim the remaining fresh foliage to size and arrange it around the wreath. Play with the design until you are happy with it before securing the foliage in place. Use a measuring tape to check that the spacing between the foliage is even.

4 Tuck individual sprigs of fresh foliage into the frame between the fir bunches. Attach other bunches of foliage with short lengths of wire, tucking the ends of the wire into the fir to hide them.

5 Arrange the dried foliage on top of the wreath to get an idea of the finished look, then glue in position.

6 Hang the wreath on a hook, or if you prefer, attach a ribbon at the top to hang it. You can scent it with a few drops of fragrance oil or leave it as it is. Spritz regularly with water to keep it fresh.

Foliage and berry wreath

This lovely, natural-looking autumnal wired wreath of complementary and harmonious colors actually includes some dyed leaves to give the best effect: the dye almost preserves the fresh leaves so they don't turn dry and brittle (although if they get wet they can stain paintwork). The base of the wreath is built up with moss, which is a better option than floral foam, as it is lighter and has more depth at the side to attach the foliage. As with all arrangements, turn the wire frame around as you pack in the moss so that the section you work on is always in front of you. Either hang the wreath, unadorned, on a wall or propped up on a mantelpiece, or attach a bow and hang it on a door. You can also lay it flat in the middle of a table and place a candle in the center. It should last for two weeks.

Flowers and foliage

- 12 dyed beech stems
- 4 dyed eucalyptus stems
- 12 miniature hebe stems
- 12 dyed oak leaf stems
- 8 pepper berry sprays
- 1 large bag sphagnum moss
- 8 unripe blackberry sprays
- 12 rosemary sprigs

Equipment

- Wire wreath frame (12 in/30 cm in diameter) from a florist
- Florist's scissors
- 1 ball of garden string
- 22 gauge wire
- Ribbon (optional)

1 Prepare the foliage: cut the stems down to 5–6 in (12–15 cm) or so and strip the leaves off the lower 1 in (2.5 cm) of each stem.

2 Position the wire frame so the larger ring lies below the smaller ring. Tie the ball of string onto the wire frame at any point and secure it in a knot. Take a large handful of moss, tease it apart slightly, and pack it in between the two rings in a rounded shape. Gather up loose ends as you press the moss into place, then wind the string diagonally around it to keep it in place. Repeat until the frame is covered.

3 Trim the moss with scissors. Cut the string, leaving a length of about 16 in (40 cm) still attached to the wreath. Make a loop in the string 4 in (10 cm) from the attached end. Hold the loop in one hand and the tail end in the other and cross them over under the wreath. Bring them back up above the wreath and tie them in a knot. Trim the loose ends.

4 If you want to hang the finished wreath, feel for the edge of the frame with your fingers and insert a length of thick wire into the moss, under the frame at an angle, and out the other side. Bring the ends together to make a loop, twist one length of wire around the other, trim the ends, and hide the twisted ends inside the moss. Holding the loop, twist the wreath around twice in the same direction to tighten the base of the loop.

5 Tie the ball of string back onto the wreath at any point. Place three to four beech leaf stems on top of the moss and wrap string tightly over the stems to secure them to the wreath. Turn the wreath around slightly and place a stem of hebe partly over the oak leaves to create a staggered effect. Secure it in place with the string.

6 Add each of the ingredients in turn, placing small bunches of foliage on the sides and top of the moss. Stagger each group of foliage and turn the wreath as you work.

7 When you have added enough foliage to give a well-balanced look, tie off the string in the same way as before: make a double loop, tuck one loop under the wreath, and tie the two single loops together securely.

8 If you spot any gaps in the wreath, or it looks slightly unbalanced in parts, tuck a few pieces of woody-stemmed foliage such as rosemary and hebe in under the string to even it out. Tie the ribbon in a bow and attach it to the frame, if using.

Mixed winter arrangement

This crisp white and green vase arrangement, with its heavy winter berries, is warmed up gently by exotic cymbidium orchids (these orchids flower on a very long stem, so the individual heads can be cut off and inserted into orchid vials to give them enough height to suit the design). Such a lovely all-around display would look stunning in a hallway, master bedroom, on a dining room table, or on a low coffee table. The soft-stemmed anemones may need replacing after a few days, but the other blooms should last up to 10 days if you keep them in good condition.

1 Place the chicken wire inside the vase and fill the vase with water.

2 Arrange the skimmia stems first. Keep turning the vase around as you add the foliage to create a fully three-dimensional domed effect. Try not to add too much foliage at this stage.

3 Add the single roses next, placing the shorter stems around the edge of the arrangement and longer ones near the center to reinforce the domed effect. The flowers should look ordered and not muddled. Keep turning the vase so it faces you as you add the roses.

4 Arrange the hypericum and spray roses next, spacing them evenly throughout the arrangement. Recess the flowers slightly so that the tips of the skimmia leaves break the curved contours of the blooms. Then add the anemones.

5 Finally, add the cymbidium orchids—they are quite dominant in this design, so it's worth arranging them last to work out where they sit best.

Flowers and foliage

- 6 white spray roses
- 5 cymbidium orchids
- 6 single white roses
- 10 hypericum berry stems
- 6 white anemones
- 10 skimmia stems

Equipment

- Opaque green glazed flared vase (7 in/19 cm high)
- Chicken wire
- Florist's scissors

Possible substitutions

Trachelium (for anemonies), mini amaryllis (for spray roses), Singapore orchids (for cymbidium orchids), berried ivy and rosemary (for skimmia)

Winter bouquet

We tend to assume that winter is bereft of plants with color and variety, but this beautiful mixed hand-tied bouquet uses species such as berried ivy as a feature rather than as a backdrop to give structure, definition, and interest (the spiral technique is the best way to control the overall shape of these very different blooms). This bouquet is ideal as a gift or as a table centerpiece in a clear glass vase at a dinner party. It will last up to ten days in water if you refresh the water and re-cut the stems.

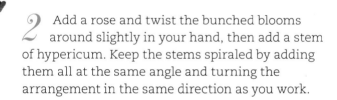

1 Sort the different ingredients into separate piles. Hold one amaryllis stem gently upright in one hand and encircle it with two or three stems of berried ivy.

2 Add a rose and twist the bunched blooms around slightly in your hand, then add a stem of hypericum. Keep the stems spiraled by adding them all at the same angle and turning the arrangement in the same direction as you work.

3 When you have added one of each of all the different ingredients, check that you are happy with the arrangement of stems by tilting it toward you, or checking it in a mirror. Trim the stems if necessary if the bouquet is becoming unwieldy in your hand. Add another amaryllis stem at an angle and continue to add the rest of the flowers and foliage.

4 Tie the arrangement securely with a length of raffia or garden string. Treat the amaryllis stems with care, as they may split under too much pressure.

5 Cut the stems at an angle so they are roughly the same length and will all be able to sit in water. If the arrangement is well balanced, it should be able to stand unaided. If the bouquet is a gift to someone, stand it in water until you present it.

Flowers and foliage

- 5 ruby red single roses
- 7 'Red Lion' amaryllis
- 5 'Tamango' spray roses
- 7 'Dolly Parton' hypericum stems
- 10 berried ivy stems

Equipment

- Florist's scissors
- Raffia or garden string

Tip

Amaryllis stems are fragile and the flower heads they carry are heavy, so the stems can easily split if you hold them too tightly. Buy stems that are as fresh as possible with the buds just opening so the flower heads don't splay out in the arrangement.

Grow a mistletoe shrub

The evergreen mistletoe plant has become an essential part of our Christmas tradition, and everyone loves its romantic connotations. The bushy shrub is actually a partial parasite that grows in the branches of old trees: it extracts essential nutrients and water by pushing its roots under the bark of the host tree. Although it is slow-growing and can be hard to establish, mistletoe is worth cultivating if you enjoy its clusters of smooth, bright green, oval leaves and waxy white berries in your home at Christmas time.

Mistletoe (Viscum album) reproduces naturally when birds —such as phainopepla—eat the berries and excrete the seeds onto the bark of a host tree, where they germinate. Popular host trees are those with soft bark, particularly apple trees, and also hawthorn, linden, and poplar trees. After attaching itself to the host, a young plant produces leaves after the first year; just two new branches with a pair of leaves at each tip grow every year.

Propagating mistletoe

The best time to propagate mistletoe is between March and April, when the seeds are fully ripe. If you can't find fresh berries from a living plant, preserve some Christmas sprigs with berries in a jar of water in the window of a cold, frost-free room until the end of February. Use the sticky "glue" of the berry to attach it to the side or underside of an apple tree branch about 8 inches (20 cm) in diameter. The higher up a tree the branch is, and the more sunlight the plant gets, the better. Wind some wool or twine around the branch to mark the site and leave the plant to establish naturally. It's worth applying 15 or more berries to your host tree, as mistletoe requires male and female plants to produce berries. The germination rate is also quite low (only one in ten seeds becomes a plant), and some berries may fall off or be eaten by birds. It will take four to five years for the plant to produce berries.

To decorate your home with mistletoe, cut a few stems from the shrub with a pair of shears, bind the base of the stems with some twine, and hang the bundle from a ceiling light or above a doorway.

Edible bird decorations

A yard full of wildlife is always an uplifting sight on a winter's day. To encourage birds into your yard, hang homemade birdseed balls from trees and shrubs. The birds rely on these additional sources of nutrients if natural foods are scarce, and in severe winter weather when snow is on the ground. Use a recycled glass tumbler as a mold if you don't have an old tennis ball.

Materials

- 18 oz (500 g) lard
- 3½ oz (100 g) coarse oats
- 3½ oz (100 g) nuts—peanuts are a good choice
- 3½ oz (100 g) dried fruits
- 3½ oz (100 g) seeds—sunflower seeds are the best choice
- Garden wire
- Old tennis ball or similar, sliced in half and with a small round hole cut out of the top, then resealed by wrapping a length of wire around the ball and twisting the wire ends together securely
- Garden string

1 Put the lard into a saucepan and melt it gently over a low heat. While the lard is melting, mix the dry ingredients together.

2 Add handfuls of the dry food to the melted lard and mix them together. The dry ingredients should all be well coated in the lard.

3 Insert a piece of wire, which is a little longer than the mold, down through the center of the mold. Pack the seed mix in around the wire.

4 Leave the seed mix in the molds to cool completely, then remove the molds, attach string to the wires, and hang the decorations up high.

Buy and recycle a real tree

For many of us, a real tree trimmed with decorations is what Christmas is all about, and it takes center stage in our homes. Looking after a cut Christmas tree properly will help to prolong its fresh scent and vibrant color, but just as important is knowing how to recycle the tree afterwards, because the benefits of recycling Christmas trees are enormous.

It takes tree farmers about ten years to produce a 10 ft (3 m) Christmas tree, and some varieties can reach great heights if left to grow: the Nordman fir (Abies nordmanniana) can reach 13 ft (40 m), for example. The best varieties to choose are Noble fir (Abies procera) and Nordman fir (Abies nordmanniana), since they have a good color and scent and hang on to their needles well, and Scots pine (Pinus sylvestris), which has the best scent.

Choosing a tree

Buy a locally grown tree to help support your community: you'll be supporting your local grower and minimizing the impact of transport miles, and you can guarantee it has been freshly cut and its needles will stay on longer. Norway Spruce (Picea abies), the "original" Christmas tree, is mostly grown in the northeastern US and may be cut down weeks before you buy it, which is why it sheds its needles quickly. Choose a species of tree that is grown locally to ensure freshness. Cut ¼–⅛ in (3–5 mm) off the base of your tree trunk, stand it in water, add a tablespoon of honey (which mimics the tree's sap), and keep the room as cool as possible to help the tree stay fresher for longer.

Recycling your tree

Currently, a large percentage of cut trees are sent to landfill sites, but recycled trees can be chipped and used to benefit the environment again as mulch, path surfacing, and soil improvers. Many communities now provide a collection site from which the trees will be properly recycled, or find out where your nearest recycling center is.

Christmas tree facts

According to the National Christmas Tree Association, live trees can be recycled and used by a number of different organizations and for a wide variety of purposes, including helping to keep erosion at bay in the coastal wetlands of Louisiana and providing nesting sites for bird populations across the country.

In the US, there are approximately 500,000 acres of land devoted to Christmas tree production. The chief Christmas-tree growing states are Oregon, North Carolina, and Michigan.

When buying a tree, consider buying a potted tree which can be used for several years before being planted outdoors.

An artificial Christmas tree may be reusable, but it will probably have been made from a petroleum-based product and may well have been flown in from China. The materials commonly used in the manufacture of artificial trees are PVC, polyurethane foam, and steel. Although you may reuse it for several years, if your tree is not recyclable it will eventually linger for centuries in a landfill site.

Christmas tree in a pot

One of the great pleasures of Christmas is decorating a real tree, so why not buy a living tree with roots and plant it in a pot? A small tree makes a great table decoration. You can re-pot it, care for it through the seasons, and reuse it for several Christmases to come. Contact a Christmas tree farm in your area and request to purchase one of their young plants.

Materials

- 1 dwarf conifer tree with the roots well soaked in a bucket of water; if you choose another variety, check on the eventual height of the tree before you buy it
- 1 container with draining holes
- Bark-based, coarse organic compost
- Watering can

Green tip

Owning a living tree
Don't keep the tree indoors for any longer than one month: the warmth and light may encourage it to break dormancy. Feed and water it regularly, re-pot into a larger container in early spring, and add some slow-release organic fertilizer, such as comfrey pellets.

1 Tease the roots of the root ball to loosen them. Fill the base of the container with some compost and place the tree in the container.

2 Pack the spaces around the root ball with more compost. Gently shake the container occasionally to distribute the compost evenly.

3 Fill the container to just below the rim with some more compost, then firm the earth around the plant with your hands.

4 Water the plant thoroughly to ensure that all the compost is wet, allow to drain, and then bring it indoors to decorate.

Natural decoration variations

Simple orange pomanders Make natural baubles by evenly scoring orange skins and slowly dehydrating the fruits.

Fruit and flower sprigs For simple, stylish decorations, tie stems of rosehips to dried teazle heads with wire and finish with a loop.

Spiced fruits Attach single fruits and dried sliced chilies with colored wire to either end of a decorated orange slice.

Frosted Christmas lanterns Use a few wispy seed heads instead of a thistle head to give decorations a frosted effect.

Citrus slices Make a hole in the top of a dried orange slice, thread through a length of string, and secure in a knot.

Cinnamon walnut bundles Attach a walnut at either end of thin rope, wrap the rope around the sticks, and glue on a star anise.

Cranberry hearts Thread thin string through dried cranberries using a needle, secure in a heart shape, and finish with a loop.

Snow clouds Tie extra quantites of wispy or fluffy seed heads to Chinese lanterns with thin wire and finish with a loop.

A flock of festive birds

These beautiful felt tree decorations are fun to make and last a lifetime. The basic method is straightforward; it's up to you how sophisticated you want the decorations and details to be. Take your inspiration from your favorite birds, and make these felt birds as colorful as you like. Make them uniquely personal by adding a family member's initials to each finished decoration.

1 Cut two body and wing shapes and some flower and leaf shapes for each bird. Make a hole in the top of each body shape with a skewer.

2 Stitch a flower eye onto the outside of each body shape at the head, then sew some flower and leaf motifs onto the body and wings.

3 Embroider simple patterns onto the felt shapes, then sew the two body shapes together using blanket stitch. Repeat with the two wing shapes.

4 Cut a slit close to the top of the bird's body and push through the sewn wings. Thread the leather strip through the hole and tie it in a loop.

Materials

- Felt in assorted colors
- Festive bird templates (pp.276–77)
- Scissors
- Skewer
- Colored embroidery thread and needle
- Leather strips or lengths of twine
- Found and recycled materials to decorate the bird (optional, see tip)

Green tip

Recycled decorations
Source a variety of items from the garden or kitchen shelves or drawers to decorate each bird. Look out for grasses, twigs, dried flowers, dried beans, rice and pasta, bay leaves, old candy wrappers, buttons, and vintage beads.

Festive bird variations
Decorate these exquisite birds in flight
with whatever foraged materials you
can find: glue on a few grass heads,
twigs, or thin ribbons to create
plumage; or sew on some recycled
sequins or vintage beads to make the
birds sparkle as they catch the light.

Recycled paper decorations

It's worth collecting all sorts of attractive or colorful recycled papers to make these child-friendly tree decorations. Look out for wallpaper samples, pages from magazines, and old oddments of wrapping paper, and recycle the cardboard from items such as tea and cereal boxes to use as the backing material for each decoration.

Materials

For each decoration

- Template (pp.278–79)
- Recycled paper in festive colors
- Recycled cardboard
- Eco-friendly adhesive glue
- Scissors
- Length of string or wool
- 1 vintage bead or button

Green tip

Eco decorations

It's worth making your own tree decorations, as bought decorations are often chemically treated, or made from non-biodegradable substances.

1 Place the template on the piece of paper and draw around it. Cut out a piece of cardboard roughly the same size as the piece of paper.

2 Glue the piece of recycled cardboard onto the back of the paper and leave to one side for a while for the glue to dry completely.

3 Cut out the paper shape neatly using a sharp pair of scissors. Trim the shape if necessary so that no pen or pencil marks are showing.

4 Thread both ends of the string through a bead or button to create a loop. Glue the string loop to the back of the card and allow to dry.

Scented fabric hearts

These pretty little filled fabric hearts look adorable hanging from a tree, but they can also be given as stocking stuffers to be hung in closets or tucked into drawers to fragrance clothes. Dried lavender flowers or natural potpourri both make ideal fillings, or fill the hearts with grains of dried rice or barley fragranced with a few drops of your favorite scented essential oil.

1 Using the template, cut out two heart shapes from the fabric. Align and sew them together around the edges, leaving a small gap on one side.

2 Snip gently around the edges of the seams with the scissors, taking care not to cut the stitching. Then turn the fabric inside out.

3 Iron the fabric to get rid of any creases, then pack the heart with the scented filling. Sew up the open gap with the needle and thread.

4 Make a knot at one end of the string and sew it onto the heart. Thread the string through the stick and leaves, knot it, and finish in a loop.

Materials

- Heart template (p.282)
- Recycled fabric (use an old gingham dish towel or tablecloth)
- Scissors or pinking shears
- Cotton thread and needle
- Your choice of filling, such as dried lavender
- Length of string
- 1 cinnamon stick with a hole through the center (use a knitting needle or skewer to do this)
- Several dried bay leaves with a hole through the center of each

Advent calendar sacks

If you want a change from the traditional, flat cardstock Advent calendars, try making these fabric sacks to hang on your Christmas tree, or use them to decorate a smaller table-top tree. They are easy to make, and can be filled with whatever treats your family enjoys—try a mixture of homemade sweets, bite-size cookies, fresh nuts, and tiny gifts.

1 Using the template, cut the cloth into 48 sack shapes. Then cut 24 small squares of fabric, each about 1¼ x 1¼ in (3 x 3 cm) in size.

2 Align two sack shapes, correct sides facing inward. Sew three sides together. Leave a seam of ½ in (1 cm). Repeat with the other shapes.

3 Mark a day of Advent, from 1 to 24, on each fabric square. Make a hole in the top corner of each square, thread through the twine, and knot it.

4 Fill each sack with a few treats, then tie the twine around the top to seal the sack. Secure the ends in a loop and hang from the tree.

Materials

- Template (p.284)
- Old tablecloth, or pretty curtain material
- Scissors or pinking shears
- Cotton needle and thread or sewing machine
- Eco-friendly marker pen
- 24 lengths of garden twine or string, each about 12½ in (32 cm) long
- Treats to fill each sack

Fabric candy cane cones

These cones look utterly irresistible when filled with sweet treats and hung from the tree. If you line the inside of each cone with a little parchment paper to protect the fabric from the sugary treats, you can use these decorations over and over again. For a more rustic effect, wrap the piece of wire around your finger and into a coil first before attaching it to the cone.

Materials

For each decoration

- A piece of cream felt (use an old felted blanket, p.16)
- Recycled fabric for lining
- Template (p.283)
- Scissors
- Pins
- Cotton thread and needle or sewing machine
- Knitting needle
- Colored embroidery thread for sewing around the rim of the cone
- A short length of recycled ribbon
- Vintage or recycled button
- Red wool (optional)
- A length of wire approximately 20 in (50 cm) long

1 Cut one cone shape from the felt and one from the lining fabric. Align and pin the fabric shapes together, correct sides facing inward.

2 Stitch the short edges together. Fold lengthwise, correct sides facing inward. Stitch the curved edges together, leaving the lining half unsewn.

3 Turn the fabric inside out through the gap in the lining using a knitting needle. Leave a band of lining showing at the top of the cone.

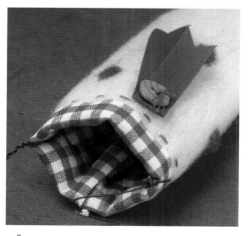

4 Sew around the rim to hold the lining in place. Decorate with a ribbon and button, or sew on red wool spots. Attach the wire at either side.

Doll pin tree angel

An old-fashioned pin doll has a nostalgic appeal that makes it a perfect decoration for any Christmas tree. If your tree is small, hang the angel right at the top of the tree, or for a larger tree make up several angels to dress the branches. Use a traditional wooden clothes pin to create the angel's body; if you can't buy any of these pins locally, try finding them on the internet.

Materials

- Recycled natural raffia
- 1 wooden clothes pin
- Eco-friendly adhesive glue
- Eco-friendly marker pen
- Old tablecloth
- Templates (p.275)
- Scissors
- Cotton thread and needle, or sewing machine
- Garden wire, about 6 in (15 cm) long
- Cream felt (p.16)
- Recycled ribbon

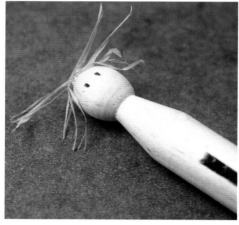

1 Attach a few short strands of raffia to the top of the clothes pin with a dab of glue. Draw two eyes onto the pin head with the marker pen.

2 Cut two shapes from the cloth using the template. Align and sew the sides of the dress together, leaving a gap in the neck to fit the pin.

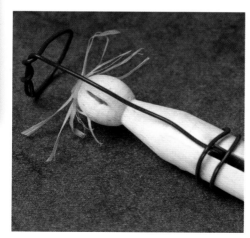

3 Twist one end of the wire into a circle. Bend the free end at right angles to the circle. Wind it around the pin to secure the halo in place.

4 Cut the wings from the felt using the template. Glue a loop of ribbon, then the dress, onto the wings. Glue the pin inside the dress.

Fabric and paper Christmas tree

These delightful decorations are all made from eco-friendly materials, such as vintage fabric (pp.52–53, 58–59), old, woollen blankets (pp.46–47, 56–57), and discarded paper (pp.50–51), and are endlessly reusable, or recyclable.

Cinnamon spice bundles

With its distinctly warm, aromatic smell, cinnamon spice can instantly create a familiar festive scent in any room. Golden-red cinnamon sticks, which are actually pieces of bark from the evergreen cinnamon tree, are easy to purchase and make striking natural decorations. Try finding long cinnamon sticks to make these spice bundles for your Christmas tree.

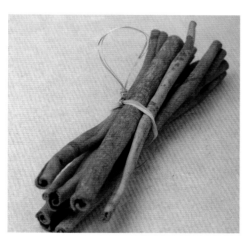

1 Secure the cinnamon sticks in a bundle with the elastic band. Thread the wire under the elastic band and secure it tightly in a loop.

2 Thread a nutmeg onto the raffia, down to one end. Tie a knot in the end of the raffia to secure the nutmeg. Repeat at the other end.

3 Wrap the raffia around the cinnamon bundle a couple of times so that the elastic band is completely hidden. Secure in a knot.

4 Glue the star anise onto the front of the orange slice, then glue the orange slice onto the raffia so that it covers the knot.

Materials

For each decoration

- 6–8 cinnamon sticks
- 1 recycled elastic band
- Length of thin wire, approximately 6 in (15 cm) long
- 2 nutmegs with a hole drilled through the center of each (use a clamp and fine-bore drill bit)
- Length of recycled natural raffia, about 20 in (50 cm) long
- Eco-friendly adhesive glue
- 1 star anise
- 1 dried orange slice

Spiced orange decorations

Even after they have been dried thoroughly, oranges retain enough of an aroma to fill a room for many days with their citrus scent. Their mellow orange hues and cylindrical shape also mean that they make naturally attractive decorations, especially when hung from the vibrant green branches of a real conifer tree.

Materials

For each decoration

- Eco-friendly adhesive glue
- 1 star anise
- 1 dried orange slice
- 1 flat, dried bay leaf
- Several lengths of thin wire
- A handful of cloves
- 1 dried, whole clementine
- Skewer or knitting needle
- 1 cinnamon stick

Craft tip

Dehydrating fruits

Arrange the slices and whole fruits in a single layer on a piece of cheesecloth on a wire rack. Leave to dry in a very low oven or a warm cabinet, which can take 48 hours or longer.

1 Glue the star anise onto the front of the orange slice, and the bay leaf onto the back. Secure a length of wire in a loop at the top of the orange.

2 Stick cloves into the clementine in a pattern. Push a skewer through the fruit, thread wire through the hole and secure one end in a loop.

3 Thread wire lengthwise through the cinnamon stick. Bend one end over, thread the other end through the clementine loop, and secure.

4 Attach the loose wire at the top of the clementine to the orange slice. The three parts should now all be joined together by wire.

Iced cookie decorations

This simple gingerbread recipe is easy to follow and makes about 35 edible tree decorations. The dough is easy to handle, so children will love rolling it, cutting out different festive shapes, and decorating the baked cookies with icing. Keep an eye on the cookies while they bake, as they may burn.

1 Preheat the oven to 375°F (190°C). Put the flour, baking soda, ginger, and cinnamon in a bowl. Rub in the butter so the mix resembles breadcrumbs. Stir in the sugar.

2 Add the egg and syrup, then mix to form a dough. Turn out onto a lightly floured surface and knead to bring the dough together.

3 Divide the dough into two batches. Roll each batch out with a lightly floured rolling pin to an even thickness of about ¼ in (5 mm).

4 Cut shapes with cookie cutters, make a hole in each with a skewer, place on greased baking trays, and bake for about 10 minutes.

Ingredients

- 3 cups all-purpose flour
- 1 tsp baking soda
- 2 tsp ground ginger
- 2 tsp ground cinnamon
- 1 stick butter, cut into pieces
- ¾ cup light unrefined sugar
- 1 egg, beaten
- 4 tbsp sugar syrup

For the icing
- 1 egg white, beaten with 5–7 oz (150–200 g) confectioner's sugar (adjust the quantity slightly, depending on the size of the egg; the icing should be smooth)

Iced cookie variations

Angel Beat the egg white and confectioner's sugar until smooth consistency. Pipe patterns to suit shapes like this angel.

Star To create repeat patterns like this star shape, ice the outside edge first and echo the shape as you work inward.

Heart Pipe on these straight and fluted lines with a piping bag or a clean, recycled plastic sandwich bag with the corner cut off.

Shooting star Reopen any holes that close during baking, then pipe icing around them to make patterns like these star shapes.

Holly leaf Press the piping bag gently and evenly with both hands as you draw on intricate details like these holly leaf berries.

Christmas tree Add organic red coloring to a separate batch of icing to make these color-contrasting tree decorations.

Snowman Change the piping bag nozzle to one with serrated edges for patterned details like the buttons on this snowman.

Candy cane Keep the patterns on slim-shaped cookies clear and simple, such as the outline and stripes on this candy cane.

Nougat sweets

These wonderfully sticky, very light soft sweets are perfect for filling tiny galvanized buckets or fabric candy cane cones, hanging from the Christmas tree. You'll need a sugar thermometer to ensure that the sugar solution reaches the correct temperature as it boils; be aware that it is extremely hot at this stage, so don't let children come too close to the pan.

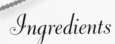

Ingredients

- 3½ cups granulated sugar
- 1½ cups sugar syrup
- ¼ cup clear honey
- 1 cup water
- 2 egg whites, beaten until stiff in a large bowl
- 1 tsp vanilla extract
- 10 oz (275 g) mixture of blanched almonds, hazelnuts, and macadamia nuts

1 Heat the sugar, syrup, honey, and water in a saucepan until it reaches 310°F (154°C). Stand thermometer in the pan to check the temperature.

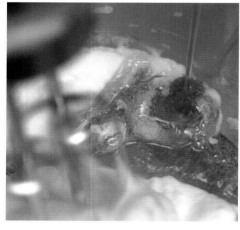

2 When the sugar solution is ready, add it to the bowl of beaten egg whites, beating the mixture constantly until it is stiff and waxy.

3 Add the vanilla extract and the nuts to the bowl and fold them all carefully into the mixture using a large metal spoon.

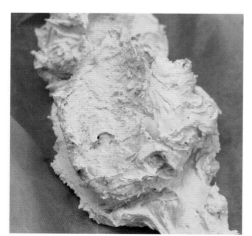

4 Put the nougat mix into a tin lined with wax paper. Allow to cool completely before cutting it into small squares. Store in an airtight tin.

Evergreen centerpiece

A special seasonal foliage centerpiece will dress your table perfectly and set the scene for a festive meal. Evergreen foliage such as bay and conifer will last well and look fresher for longer than some other seasonal varieties, but choose whatever you have available in the yard, or can buy, to make the best-looking table display.

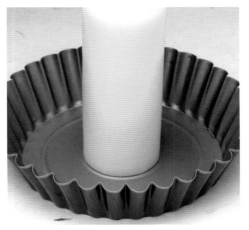

Materials

- Deep, fluted baking dish
- 1 large candle
- Small bunches of evergreen foliage, such as bay and conifer
- Shears
- Thin garden wire
- A few pine cones

1 Place the baking dish on a flat, level surface. Use a dish with a fixed, rather than a removable, base, so that water won't leak out of it.

2 Position the candle in the center of the dish. If you wish, you can stick the candle into place, but use a waterproof glue to do this.

3 Cut the conifer foliage into small bundles using shears. Tie wire around each bundle and place them in the dish around the candle.

4 Insert other foliage in between the conifer bundles. Position the pine cones around the candles and add a little water to keep the foliage fresh.

Herb variation

Gather a selection of fresh, seasonal herbs such as rosemary, sage, thyme, and bay leaves, and use them to create an alternative table centerpiece (pp.72–73).

Fresh foliage variation
Pick a selection of whatever fresh foliage and winter flowers you may have growing in your winter garden for this variation on the evergreen centerpiece (pp.72–73).

Individual setting variations

Rosemary and sage Place a few sprigs of rosemary in a tiny galvanized bucket, tuck in a sage stem, and add a little water.

Bay leaf, thyme, and rosemary Place thyme and rosemary sprigs in a tiny bucket and insert three bay leaves in a row.

Ivy and red berries Fill an egg cup with sprigs of bright red berries and tuck in a few short lengths of ivy around the edge.

Rosehips, ivy, and moss Put a few slightly longer rosehip stems in an egg cup and pack moss and ivy leaves around them.

Fresh flowers Cut fresh flowers from plants that flourish in a winter garden, such as Christmas rose (Helleborus niger), Lenten rose (Helleborus orientalis), or witch hazel (Hamamellis mollis). Put them in a small foil-lined box or pot, and add a little water.

Painting glass techniques

Glass painting is an inexpensive craft that requires minimal tools and materials. It is a great way to recycle old glassware and give it a new lease on life. Clear glass is the most versatile for painting on, but also consider colored and frosted glass. Glass paint applied to frosted glass will make it transparent. Practice painting on acetate or an old piece of glass before starting on a project.

Making a template for a straight-sided or conical container

1 Slip a piece of tracing paper inside a straight-sided or conical container. Adjust the paper so that it rests against the glass, then tape it in place. Mark the position of the overlap and the upper edge with a pencil.

2 Remove the tracing paper and cut out the template along the overlap and upper edge. Transfer your design onto the tracing paper with a black pen. Stick the tracing under the glass with masking tape, butting the side edges of the template together.

Sticking a template under a double curvature

1 Templates to be used on rounded glassware need to be adapted to fit the shape. Make cuts into the template with a pair of scissors.

2 Tape the template under the glass at the top and bottom. The cuts will overlap or spread open to fit the curves of the glassware.

Transferring a design

1 If the aperture is too small to stick a template inside, the design can be transferred to the outer surface of the glass with a grease pencil. Turn the tracing over and redraw the lines with a grease pencil.

2 Tape the template, grease-pencil-side down, on the glass. Draw over the lines again with a sharp standard writing pencil to transfer the design onto the glass. Remove the template.

Applying outliner

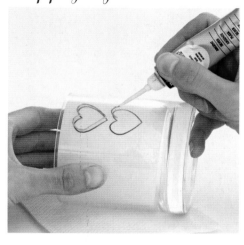

1 Resting the piece on a paper towel and with the template in place, squeeze the tube of outliner, gently drawing it along the outline of the design. Leave to dry, then turn the piece to continue.

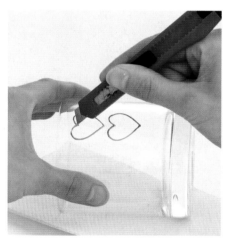

2 Wipe away major mistakes immediately with a paper towel. When dry, neaten any blobs with a craft knife. Once painted, the viewer's eye will be drawn to the painted areas and not the outliner, so don't overdo the neatening.

Painting on glass

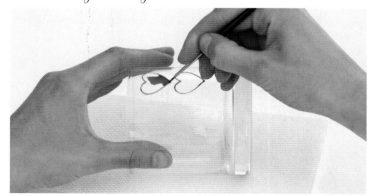

1 Resting the piece on a paper towel, apply the glass paint generously with a medium paintbrush. Use a fine paintbrush to push the paint into any corners. If working on a curve, keep the glass steady to avoid the paint running to one side.

2 To blend one color into another, apply both colors to the glass, then mix them together where they meet, making sure that the paint reaches the edge of the outliner. Leave to dry, then turn the glass to continue painting.

Tea light holder

Make a set of pretty painted tea light holders in warm shades of red and orange, outlined in gold. Candlelight will enhance the painted blossoms as it shines through the transparent glass paint. Use simple motifs in different combinations to give individuality to a set of tea light holders. For a delicate finishing touch, decorate the motifs with tiny dots applied with outliner.

Materials

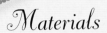

- straight-sided clear glass tea light holder
- tracing paper
- scissors
- pencil
- ruler
- black felt-tip pen
- masking tape
- paper towel
- gold outliner
- piece of white paper
- orange, red, and yellow transparent glass paints
- medium and fine artist's paintbrushes

1 Make a template and divide it into fifths. Trace a blossom and leaf motif onto each section ¼ in (6 mm) below the upper edge with the felt-tip pen. Tape the template inside the tea light holder with masking tape.

2 Resting the tea light holder on its side on a paper towel, trace the uppermost motif with gold outliner. Leave to dry. Turn the tea light holder and repeat to outline all the motifs. Remove the template when the outliner has dried.

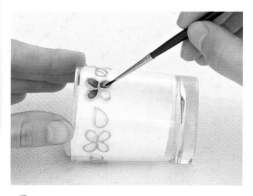

3 Slip a piece of white paper inside the tea light holder to show up the area being painted. Apply orange paint to the outer edge of the petals with a medium paintbrush. Apply red paint to the inner edge with a fine paintbrush. Blend the colors at the center. Leave to dry. Clean the paintbrushes.

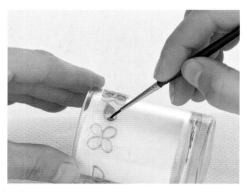

4 Apply yellow paint to the pointed end of a leaf with a clean fine paintbrush. Apply orange paint to the rounded end with a medium paintbrush. Blend the colors at the center of the leaf. Leave to dry, then turn the glass and continue painting.

5 When the last motif is dry, apply a dot of gold outliner at the center of the flower to neaten it. Apply three tiny dots along the center of the petals, then five dots along the leaf. Repeat on all the motifs. Leave the outliner to dry.

Glass jar candleholders

Candles are essential at Christmas time as they bring an extra sense of warmth, so dot these pretty tealight candleholders around a table or along a windowsill and light the candles as dusk falls. Decorate the jars with leaves and seed heads, or other simple decorations, and tie on ribbons that echo the colors in your room. Don't leave these candles unattended.

Materials

- Several recycled jam jars, baby-food jars, or similiar
- Strong wire
- Selection of leaves and seed heads, either fresh or dried
- Eco-friendly adhesive glue
- Recycled ribbon
- Several tealights

Green tip

Recycle old candles
Heat waste candles in a pan over a gentle heat. Lift out the dead wicks and cut a new wick just longer than your mold (try using an old teacup or glass). Soak in the wax. Pour the wax into the lightly oiled mold, ensuring the wick is at the center. Leave to set.

1 Clean the jars thoroughly and dry them. Put the lids aside. Cut a length of wire just larger than the diameter of the neck of a jar.

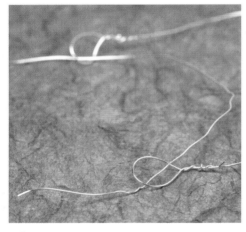

2 Cut a second length of wire about 12 in (30 cm) long. Make a secure loop at either end. Thread the first length of wire through each loop.

3 Wrap the short length of wire around the neck of the jar and secure it tightly. Adjust the loops so that the wire handle works correctly.

4 Glue leaves or seed heads onto the sides of the jar. Tie a ribbon around the neck and slip a tealight into the jar. Then decorate other jars.

Terra-cotta pot candleholders

Turn three simple terra-cotta pots into stylish candleholders: line the base of each with recycled aluminum foil, put a beeswax candle in the center, pack sand around each candle, and cover the sand with a pretty arrangement of fresh foliage and bright berries.

Decorated chair backs

These simple arrangements, made up of a few stems of trailing ivy (Hedera), mistletoe (Viscum album), and holly (Ilex), roughly tied together with natural raffia, and attached to the back of each chair, will lend a lovely rustic detail to your decorated table.

2

Personal Gifts

Soap-making techniques

The basic technique of soap-making involves melting a soap base and re-molding it into bars or slabs filled with your own custom scents, colors, and additives. Once you have mastered these basics, you can branch out to create highly decorative soaps using techniques such as layering and embedding. The only limit is your imagination.

Preparing the soap base

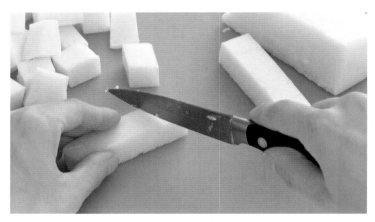

1 Weigh out enough soap base to fill your molds, allowing a little extra for wastage. Average-sized bars usually require 3–3½ oz (80–100 g) of soap. If you're not sure how much soap your mold requires, try cutting a slab to fit it.

2 Use a sharp knife to slice the soap into 1 in (2.5 cm) chunks. As a rule, the smaller and more regular the pieces, the more quickly and evenly the soap will melt.

Melting the soap base

1 To melt soap on the stove, place it in a heatproof bowl over a pan of simmering water until the soap becomes fully liquid. Stir occasionally, but try to avoid generating air bubbles.

2 Small batches of soap can be melted in the microwave. Place the soap in a microwave-proof bowl and heat on full power for a series of 10-second bursts until the soap becomes fully liquid. Never overheat or boil the soap. It only needs to be warm enough to melt.

Coloring the soap

1 Liquid dyes and pigments should be added in tiny increments to the melted soap. Use the tip of a toothpick to add color, one drop at a time.

2 If the color isn't quite strong enough, add a little more dye and stir until it is fully incorporated into the melted soap.

3 Add powdered pigment to a small batch of the melted soap and stir to dissolve it. Then incorporate this with the rest of the melted soap, little by little.

4 For intense, jewellike colors, combine transparent soap base with liquid dyes or pigment. For flatter, paler shades, use opaque soap base with liquid or powdered colorants.

Scenting the soap

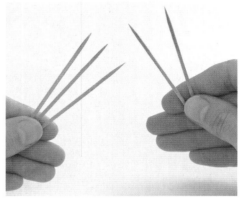

1 Add essential oils and fragrances to the soap just before molding to minimize evaporation from heat. For small batches, add the oil drop by drop until the aroma is as desired.

2 For larger batches, measure out the fragrance into a beaker. Aim for 2–3% of the total weight of the soap, or 2–3 tsp (10–15 ml) per 1 lb 2 oz (500 g) of soap.

3 When blending scents, experiment with top, middle, and base notes. Putting different combinations of dipped toothpicks in a plastic bag is a good way to play with scent blends.

Enhancing soaps with natural ingredients

1 To add a luxurious, creamy texture to opaque soap, stir in a small portion of a solid moisturizing oil such as shea butter while the soap is melting. Do not exceed $\frac{1}{5}$ oz (5 g) per 3½ oz (100 g) of soap.

2 For an exfoliating soap, stir in a handful of finely ground oatmeal into the melted soap before molding. Dried calendula or safflower petals can also be used to create a colorful, mottled texture.

3 For a decorative flourish, place slices of dried citrus fruit in the bottom of the mold and make them adhere by pouring a very thin layer of soap on top. After a minute or two, spritz with rubbing alcohol then pour in the rest of the soap.

Molding and storing soap

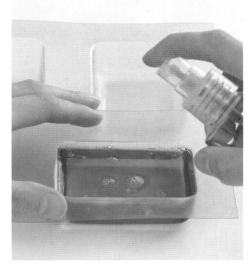

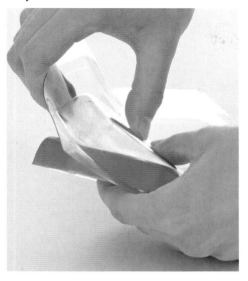

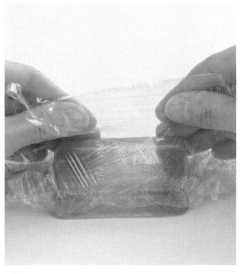

1 Once all the additives are in place, carefully pour the soap into the molds. It is common for surface bubbles to appear after pouring; these can be dissolved by spritzing immediately with rubbing alcohol. Leave to set.

2 After several hours, turn the mold upside down and flex each edge gently to release the soap. If the soap is stubborn, place it in the freezer for 15 minutes and try again. Once unmolded, slabs can be sliced into bars using a knife or metal scraper.

3 If the soap is not for immediate use, store it in plastic wrap to prevent its high glycerine content from attracting humidity in the atmosphere and "sweating."

Layering and embedding

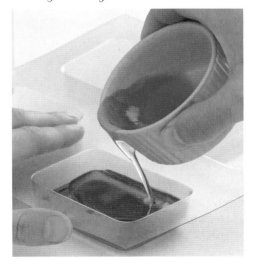

1 It is possible to create bars with multiple colors or scents by pouring in separate layers. Spritz the surface of the soap with rubbing alcohol immediately after pouring, then leave to set. Spritz again before pouring the next layer.

2 Another popular technique is to embed small pieces of contrasting soap into the center of the soap bars. These may be anything from simple, hand-cut shapes to decorative centerpieces, created with chocolate molds or cookie cutters.

3 To create the finished bar, chill the centerpieces in the freezer for at least 30 minutes and then work as you would to layer the soap, placing the centerpieces in the middle layer of the soap. Spritz each layer with rubbing alcohol before pouring the next.

Botanical soap

Have you ever wandered around a craft market and admired the array of rough-cut, rustic-looking, natural soaps that are on offer? You too can produce your very own slab of soothing lavender soap that can be cut up into bars and shared with friends. The same approach can be used with a wide range of dried herbs, flower petals, and essential oils.

Materials

- 1 cup of dried lavender buds
- 1 lb 7 oz (650 g) goat's milk soap base, chopped into small pieces
- 3 tsp (15 ml) lavender essential oil

Equipment

- pestle and mortar or food processor
- heatproof bowl
- saucepan
- metal spoon
- small measuring beaker
- Plastic container (approx 5 x 7 in/12.5 x 18 cm)
- metal scraper or knife

1 Divide the lavender buds into two equal portions. Finely grind one of the portions using a pestle and mortar or a food processor. Set aside.

2 Place the soap pieces in a heatproof bowl over a saucepan of simmering water and heat gently, stirring occasionally with a metal spoon until the soap has melted. Remove from the heat.

3 Add the lavender essential oil and the ground lavender and stir constantly for 1–2 minutes. This will help the lavender to remain evenly suspended within the soap. Allow the soap to cool slightly without setting.

4 Pour the mixture into the container. Before the soap starts to form a skin, immediately sprinkle on the unground lavender buds, and press gently with your fingers to help them adhere to the surface.

5 Allow to set for several hours before
unmolding and slicing into smaller
blocks using a metal scraper or knife.

All natural luxury soap

Handmade soaps make indulgent gifts, and using the melt-and-pour method they require no specialized skill to make. Create naturally scented and colored soaps using spices, dried fruits or flowers, essential oils, and soap colorant.

1 Wearing gloves, chop the melt-and-pour soap into pieces and heat in a heatproof bowl over a pan of boiling water, stirring occasionally, until all lumps have melted.

2 Add the desired amount of colorant to the melted soap base and stir until the powder has mixed in and the color is evenly distributed.

3 Add the lemon peel granules a little at a time, stirring gently. Continue stirring until the granules are spread evenly throughout the soap mixture.

4 Just before you pour the soap mixture into the mold, slowly add the essential oil and stir gently until it is evenly distributed throughout.

Materials

Makes 9 bars

- 1 kg (2¼ lb) white melt-and-pour soap base
- ¼–¾ tsp yellow natural mineral colour
- dried lemon peel granules
- lemon essential oil
- surgical spirit in a spray bottle
- 9 dried lemon slices
- clingfilm

Equipment

- gloves
- heatproof bowl
- pan
- spatula
- spoon
- square mould
- knife

5 Pour approximately three-quarters of the mixture into the mold. Leave the remainder in the bowl over the hot water to keep it melted and warm.

6 Spray the mixture with rubbing alcohol to remove any bubbles. Let this first layer stand for 20–25 minutes, until it is almost set. It should be hard but warm.

7 Spray the almost-set layer again with rubbing alcohol. This will act as a glue and help it to bond to the next layer of soap.

8 Slowly pour the remaining mixture into the mold and add the dried lemon slices. You will need to act fast because the top layer will begin to set as soon as it is poured.

9 Create a 3 x 3 pattern so that each bar of soap will contain a lemon slice. Spritz the surface with rubbing alcohol to remove any bubbles and let stand until hard.

10 Remove the soap from the mold and cut it with a knife into nine even squares. Wrap each square in plastic wrap to prevent it from attracting moisture.

Soap recipe variations

Bergamot soap ¼–¾ teaspoon (1–3 g) orange soap colorant, 2¼ teaspoons (10 g) bergamot essential oil, 9 whole dried orange slices.

Rose soap 2¼ teaspoons (10 g) rose absolute diluted in 5% grapeseed oil, 4 oz (100 g) rosebuds.

Cinnamon soap ¼–¾ teaspoon (1–3 g) caramel soap colorant, 2¼ teaspoons (10 g) cinnamon leaf essential oil, 9 cinnamon sticks.

Camomile soap ¼–¾ teaspoon (1–3 g) dark green soap colorant, 2¼ teaspoons (10 g) camomile essential oil, 1–1½ oz (35 g) dried camomile flowers.

Lavender soap ¼–¾ teaspoon (1–3 g) purple soap colorant, 2¼ teaspoons (10 g) English lavender essential oil, ½ oz (10 g) dried lavender.

Vanilla soap ¼–¾ teaspoon (1–3 g) cream soap colorant, 2¼ teaspoons (10 g) vanilla essential oil, 3 vanilla beans, (use seeds in the mixture).

Juniper soap ¼–¾ teaspoon (1–3 g) pink soap colorant, 2¼ teaspoons (10 g) juniper essential oil, 4 oz (100 g) juniper berries.

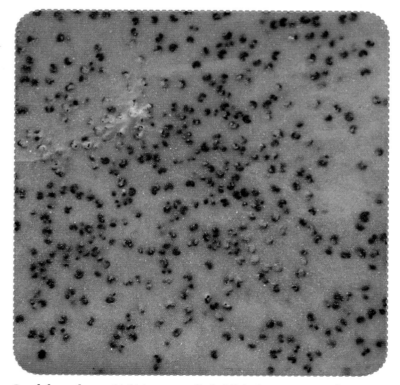

Sandalwood soap ¼–¾ teaspoon (1–3 g) light-brown soap colorant, 2¼ teaspoons (10 g) sandalwood fragrance, 2oz (50 g) blue poppy seeds.

Soap variations

Juniper cake-slice soap

You will need

- 2 lb (1 kg) white melt-and-pour soap base
- ¼ teaspoon pink soap colorant
- 2¼ teaspoons (10 g) juniper essential oil
- 4 oz (100 g) juniper berries

This soap cake is made like the lemon soap on pp.95–97, but in two stages. First, melt half the soap, adding the pink colorant and half the essential oil. Pour it into a round container and let it set, spritzing it with rubbing alcohol to get rid of any bubbles. Melt the second half of the soap, adding the remaining scent. Spritz the base again, then pour on the second layer of soap. Add the juniper berries to the top, spritzing it one final time to get rid of any remaining bubbles. Once set, remove from the mold and cut into slices.

Molded vanilla stars

You will need

- 2 lb (1 kg) white melt-and-pour soap base
- ¼–¾ teaspoon cream soap colorant
- 2¼ teaspoons (10 g) vanilla essential oil
- 3 vanilla beans, cut in pieces

These vanilla-scented stars are made in the same way as the lemon soap (pp.95–97), but the mixture is poured into individual molds to set. Soap molds are sold in craft stores, or you can use silicone cake molds. Vanilla seeds are used instead of lemon peel granules as an exfoliant and for added scent. Vanilla beans can also be used to decorate the tops of the stars by placing them into the mold before the mixture is poured on top.

Cookie-cutter lavender hearts

You will need

- 2 lb (1 kg) white melt-and-pour soap base
- ¼–¾ teaspoon purple soap colorant
- 2¼ teaspoons (10 g) lavender essential oil
- ¼ oz (10 g) dried lavender

These heart-shaped soaps are made using the same method and quantity of ingredients as the lemon soap on pp.95–97, swapping in the ingredients above. However, instead of cutting the soap into squares, they are cut with heart-shaped cookie cutters. The lavender buds will float to the top, creating an exfoliating layer.

See-through orange soap

You will need

- 2 lb (1 kg) clear melt-and-pour soap base
- 2¼ teaspoons (10 g) bergamot essential oil
- 9 dried orange slices

Although made in the same way as the lemon soap on pp.95–97, using a clear soap base and adding a dried orange slice inside the soap gives these soaps a fresh look. Make them by first melting half of the clear soap base and adding half of the essential oil. Pour the mixture into a square mold, then add the orange slices evenly to the top. Allow this layer to set before melting the remaining half of the soap base and adding the remaining essential oil. Spritz the set layer with rubbing alcohol and add the melted soap mixture to the top. Spritz again to get rid of any bubbles and allow to set. Cut the soap into nine square bars.

Fizzy bath bombs

Bath bombs are solid balls that fizz and bubble as they dissolve, adding scent and color to the bathwater. They make wonderful gifts and are surprisingly easy to make with ingredients that are readily available in most supermarkets.

1 Measure the baking soda and sift it into the larger mixing bowl.

2 Add the citric acid to the baking soda and mix well with your fingers until thoroughly combined.

3 Split the mixture between the two smaller bowls. Add the colorant to the first bowl and mix well with a spoon or your fingers, ensuring that no lumps remain.

4 Add approximately half the fragrance to the first bowl and half to the second bowl. Mix each bowl well, again making sure that no lumps remain.

Materials

Makes 1 bath bomb

- ¾ cup baking soda
- ⅓ cup citric acid
- ¼ teaspoon (1 g) purple soap colorant
- ½ teaspoon juniper essential oil
- water in a spray bottle

Equipment

- strainer
- 1 medium-sized mixing bowl
- 2 small mixing bowls
- spoon
- bath bomb mold

5 Spray both bowls lightly with water and mix it in evenly with your fingers. Continue to spritz and mix until the mixture feels damp but not too moist.

6 Fill one of the mold halves halfway with the purple mixture. Gently press the mixture down into the mold with your fingers to remove any pockets of air.

7 Add white mixture to the mold half, leaving a mound at the top. Repeat the process for the other mold half, this time starting with the white mixture.

8 Bring the two mold halves together, making sure that the two halves of the bath bomb are lined up exactly. Press the halves together.

9 Leave the bath bomb to set for approximately five minutes. Try not to move it at all during this time because it can be very fragile before it is set.

10 Once set, first remove one of the mold halves. Then place your palm over the bath bomb and gently turn it over. Remove the other mold half.

Relaxing bath oil

This simple organic bath oil recipe can be easily adapted to make a luxuriously soothing bath oil or an invigorating bath oil, just by changing the essential oils you use. Package the bottled oils in a recycled box lined with colored tissue papers and include some of the ingredients for a rustic finish, or simply tie a length of beautiful vintage ribbon around the neck of each bottle.

Materials

- 2fl oz (50 ml) sweet almond oil
- 10 drops of sandalwood essential oil
- 5 drops of jasmine essential oil
- 5 drops of orange essential oil

Equipment

- 1 pretty recycled bottle and lid, sterilize
- 1 label

For Soothing bath oil

- 10 drops of rose essential oil
- 5 drops of chamomile essential oil
- 5 drops of lavender essential oil

For Invigorating bath oil

- 10 drops of grapefruit essential oil
- 5 drops of lemon essential oil
- 5 drops of juniper essential oil

1 Carefully decant the almond oil from a measuring cup into the sterilized bottle.

2 Add each of the different essential oils, drop by drop, to the almond oil in the bottle.

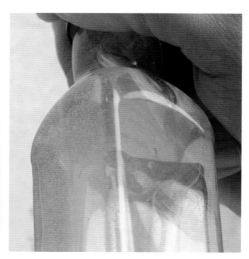

3 Screw on the lid firmly and shake the bottle until the ingredients are well blended.

4 Attach a label identifying the oil, and with instructions to add 1 tablespoon of the oil to a warm bath.

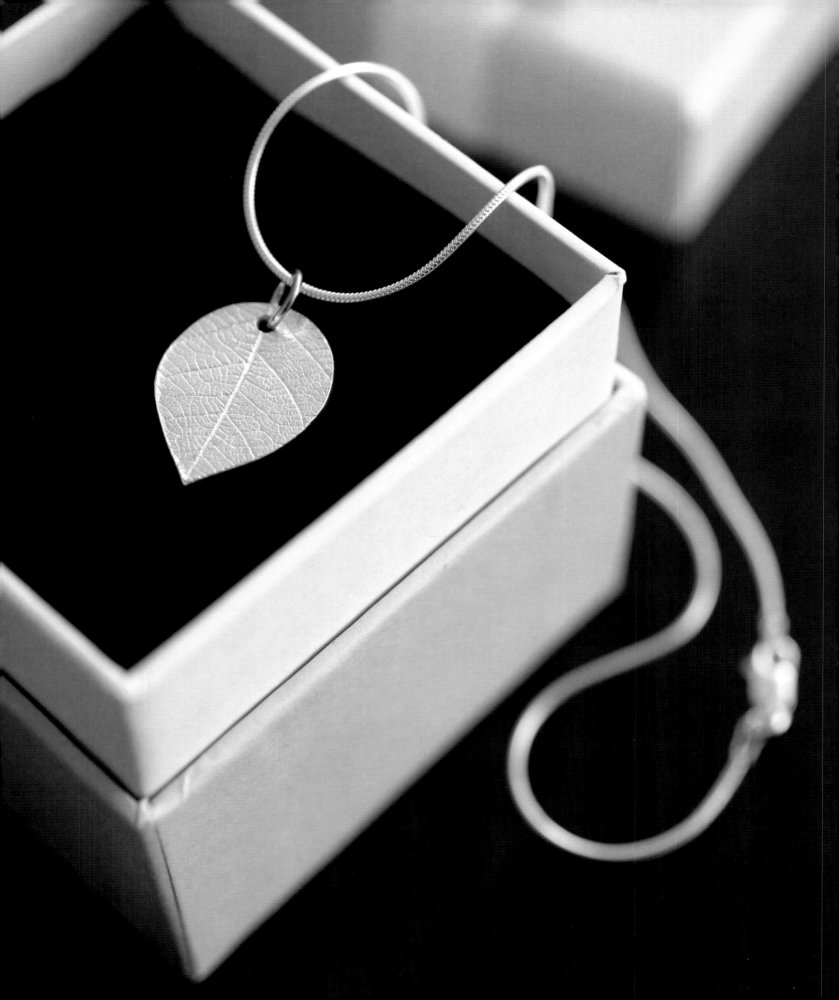

Silver clay jewelry

Make beautiful silver jewelry items easily with silver clay.
Available from craft stores, silver clay is 99% silver. When fired with
a kitchen torch, the clay burns off, leaving behind a fully silver item.

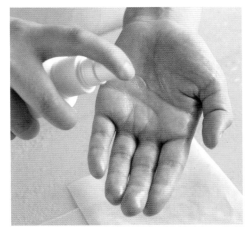

1 Cut out a square of parchment paper or use a Teflon mat. Prepare your work surface by applying a small amount of oil over the paper or mat, your hands, and the rolling pin.

2 Place two stacks of four playing cards, each about 2 in (5 cm) away from each other to act as rolling guides. Soften the clay in your hands and roll it flat.

3 Lift up the rolled clay carefully and place a leaf underneath and on top of it as shown, making sure you line up the stems and tips of the leaves. Roll over the clay again to imprint both sides.

4 Carefully remove the leaves, and lay the clay on a cutting mat or cutting board. Using the craft knife and the template from p.285, carefully cut a leaf shape from the clay.

Materials

- oil (cooking spray is ideal)
- ¼ oz (7 g) silver clay
- real leaves or leaf skeletons
- silver jump ring

Equipment

- Teflon mat or parchment paper
- small rolling pin or piece of pipe
- playing cards
- craft knife
- small straw
- wet and dry sandpaper (600 grit) or sanding pad (220 grit)
- kitchen torch
- firing brick or ceramic tile
- timer
- tweezers
- soft wire brush
- 2 pairs of pliers

5 Using the straw, make a hole in the leaf about ¼ in (5 mm) from the top. This needs to be big enough for your jump ring, bearing in mind that the clay may shrink by up to 10% when fired.

6 Let the clay dry overnight, or, to speed up the process, use a hair dryer or put the clay in an oven at 300°F (150°C) for 10 minutes. Once dry, sand it very carefully to smooth the edges.

7 Place the leaf on the firing brick or tile in a dimly lit, well ventilated room. Hold the torch 2 in (5 cm) from the clay and move the flame evenly over it. The leaf will start to glow a peachy orange color.

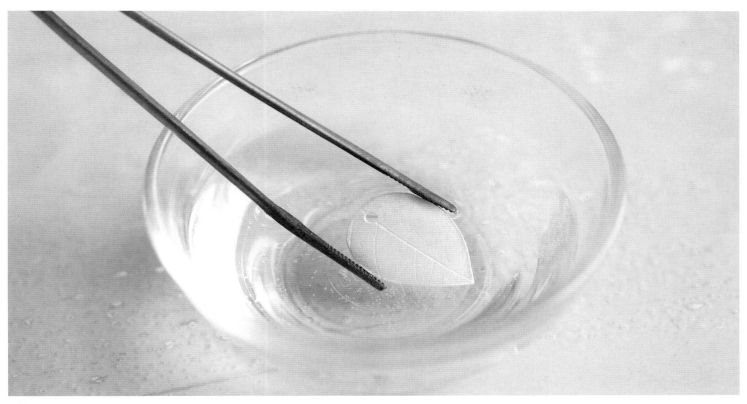

8 Once the leaf begins to glow, set the timer for two minutes. If the leaf turns bright red or shiny silver, it is too hot—move the flame away. Once fired, pick up the leaf with tweezers and quench it in water.

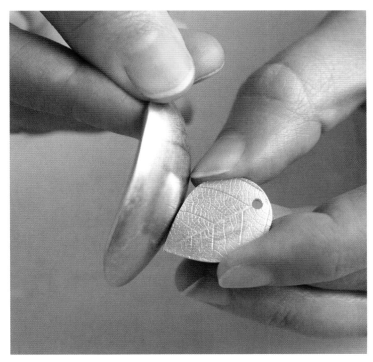

9 The leaf will now be a matte-white color, even though it is pure silver. Gently brush it with a soft wire brush to reveal the silver color. To achieve a high shine, rub with the back of a metal spoon.

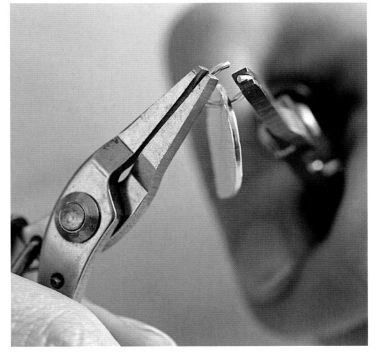

10 Using two pairs of pliers, gently twist the ends of the jump ring away from each other. Thread it through the hole in your leaf, and then twist the jump ring closed.

Silver jewelry variations

Wallpaper earrings

Patterned wallpaper can be ideal for texturing metal clays, and the variety of designs available is huge. Make these earrings using the same technique as for the silver leaf pendant on pp.109–11, using ½ oz (15 g) of silver clay. Using the wallpaper, roll and texture your clay as before. Cut ovals from the clay approximately 1¼ in (3 cm) in length using the template on p.285 and pierce at the top with your straw. Dry out, and torch fire. Burnish for a high shine, and attach ear wires.

Simple button cufflinks

A wide array of textured paper is available from most craft stores; a snakeskin pattern has been used to create these cufflinks made according to the same technique as the silver leaf pendant on pp.109–11 and using the template on p.285. To make, roll out and texture approximately ¾ oz (20 g) of silver clay. Carefully cut out two disks measuring ¾ in (2 cm) in diameter, and another two of ⅝ in (1.5 cm) in diameter. Pierce each of these disks twice using a toothpick (the holes should be positioned to resemble the holes in a button). Dry out and fire the clay as for the silver leaf pendant. Burnish for a high shine, then, using a needle and silver thread, sew the silver clay buttons onto a cufflink chain: ⅝–¾ in (1.5–2 cm) of chain with roughly ¼ in (5 mm) links is ideal. Tie off the thread, and use a tiny dot of superglue to ensure the end doesn't come loose.

Leaf bracelet

This simple leaf bracelet requires approximately 1 oz (25 g) of silver clay. Roll and texture your clay as for the silver leaf pendant on pp.109–11. Then cut out seven pointed ellipses 1 in (2.5 cm) in length. Pierce each end of the ellipses with your straw. While the pieces of clay are still soft, lay them over a rolling pin to give them a curved shape. Let them dry, and then torch fire as before. Link the elements together using jump rings. Finally, attach a simple clasp.

Lace heart key ring

Fabrics, in particular lace, can be used to produce beautifully delicate patterns in metal clays. To make this heart key ring in the same way as the silver leaf pendant on pp.109–11, roll out approximately ⅜ oz (10 g) of silver clay. Texture it using lace, and then cut out a heart shape 1⅜ in (3.5 cm) in length using the template on p.285. Pierce the top of the heart with your straw. Dry out and fire the clay, then burnish to a high shine. Use a jump ring to attach the heart to a key ring and chain.

Crochet basics

Use this quick-reference guide to (re)familiarize yourself with four basic crochet stitches. These are adapted slightly to make the crochet projects in this book.

Chain stitch (ch)

  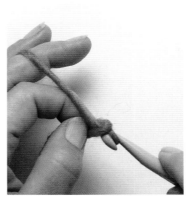

1 Make a slip knot. Hold the slip knot firmly between finger and thumb.

2 Wrap the yarn over the hook (called "yarn over" or "yo") and catch it with the hook.

3 Pull the hook and yarn back through the stitch.

4 The chain stitch is complete. Repeat steps 2–4 to continue the chain. Count the "V" shapes to count the chains.

Slip stitch (ss)

Pull the yarn through

One stitch left on the hook

With one loop on the hook, hook into the next stitch, catch the yarn and pull the loop through the stitch and loop in one movement.

Crochet necklace

This beautiful necklace is a great crochet project for beginners because it uses just one stitch—the chain stitch. For a quick lesson on how to make the stitch, turn to Crochet basics on p.114 before starting work on the necklace.

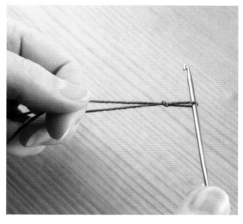

1 Make a slip knot by first crossing the yarn coming from the ball over itself to form a circle. Insert the B/1 (2 mm) hook through the circle and pull the ball end through the circle. Tighten.

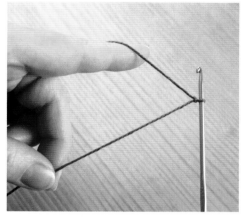

2 Pull both ends of the yarn firmly to tighten the slip knot around the shank of the hook, making sure that the knot is tight but not so tight that you can't move it along the hook.

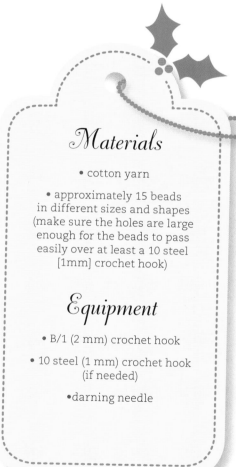

Materials

• cotton yarn

• approximately 15 beads in different sizes and shapes (make sure the holes are large enough for the beads to pass easily over at least a 10 steel [1mm] crochet hook)

Equipment

• B/1 (2 mm) crochet hook

• 10 steel (1 mm) crochet hook (if needed)

• darning needle

3 To begin the foundation chain, wrap the yarn from the ball around the hook. This action is called a "yarn over" (abbreviated yo). Use the lip of the hook to grip the yarn as shown.

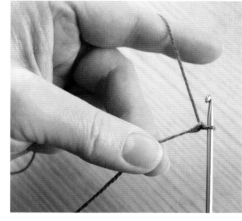

4 With the lip of the hook, pull the yarn through the loop on the shank of the hook and tighten it. This makes the first chain of your foundation chain.

5 Yo and draw a loop through the loop on the shank of the hook for the next chain. Continue making chains in this way, making a total of 10 to start.

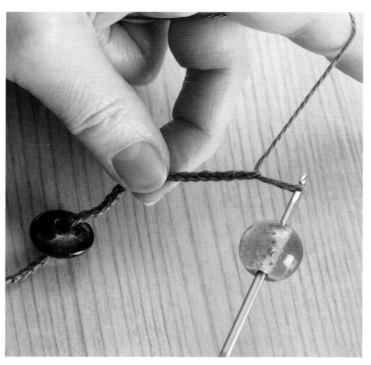

6 Thread a bead onto the hook and insert it back through the loop.

7 Pass the bead onto the loop, pulling the loop through it. If necessary, use a 10 steel (1 mm) hook for this step.

8 If you switched hooks in Step 6, switch back to the B/1 (2 mm) hook. Yo. Grasp the yarn going to the ball with the lip of the hook (see Step 3).

9 Pull the yarn through the loop to secure the bead in place. Continue chaining and adding beads in this way until the necklace is the length you require.

10 Make a slip stitch (ss) (see p.114) in the first chain to join the necklace ends. Cut the yarn, leaving a tail. Pass the tail through the last loop and tighten to finish.

11 Using a darning needle, work both yarn tails through the chains on each side of the last ss to finish.

Jewelry case

This slim case makes the perfect gift box for jewelry and other small items likely to slip out of a looser box. Wrap your gift in tissue paper and close the box with a ribbon tied in a bow to ensure that it stays safe until opened.

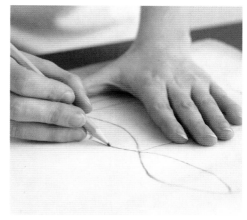

1 Use a photocopier to resize the template on p.290, if necessary. Transfer it onto a sheet of card stock using tracing paper and a pencil.

2 Flip the card stock over. Glue a sheet of tissue paper or decorative paper to the card stock, making sure that it is stuck down completely. You can also use patterned card stock.

3 Using a craft knife and a cutting mat, cut around the outside lines of the box. Make sure not to cut into the folding lines.

4 Using a ruler and one side of a pair of scissors, or a blunt knife, score along all the internal folding lines. You can erase the pencil lines at this point.

Materials

- card stock
- tracing paper
- tissue paper
- glue stick

Equipment

- pencil
- craft knife
- cutting mat
- ruler
- blunt knife (or pair of scissors)
- rubber

5 Fold the side flap up and spread glue on the patterned side. Fold the case in half and attach the flap to the inside of the opposite edge. Hold it in place until it sticks.

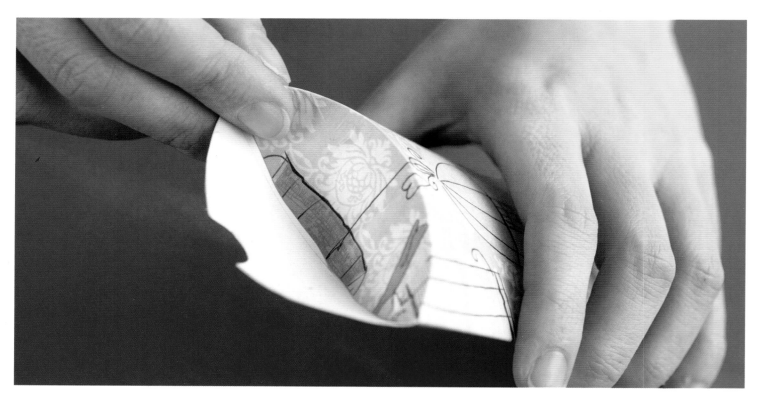

6 Choose one end to be the bottom of the case. Fold in the first flap along the curved line, and then the other. Fill the box and fold in the flaps at the other end to close.

Pyramid boxes

These small boxes are quick and easy to make, requiring no gluing at all. They are the ideal size for a small gift, or to hold candy or party favors. Personalize your boxes by using different colors and types of ribbon.

Materials

- patterned card stock (or patterned paper glued onto card stock)
- tracing paper
- ribbon

Equipment

- pencil
- craft knife
- cutting mat
- blunt knife (or pair of scissors)
- eraser
- hole punch

1 Use a photocopier to resize the template on p.291, if required. Using tracing paper and a pencil, transfer it onto a sheet of patterned card stock (or glue decorative paper to the card stock).

2 Using a craft knife and a cutting mat, cut around the outside of the box template. Make sure not to cut into the internal folding lines.

3 Lightly score along the fold lines using a ruler and a blunt knife (or one side of a pair of scissors).

4 Add a hole to the tip of each triangle using a hole punch. Try to keep them evenly spaced and make sure they are not too close to the edges in any direction.

5 For a neat finish, erase the fold lines. Fold each section and flap along the scored lines, making sure that each crease is sharp.

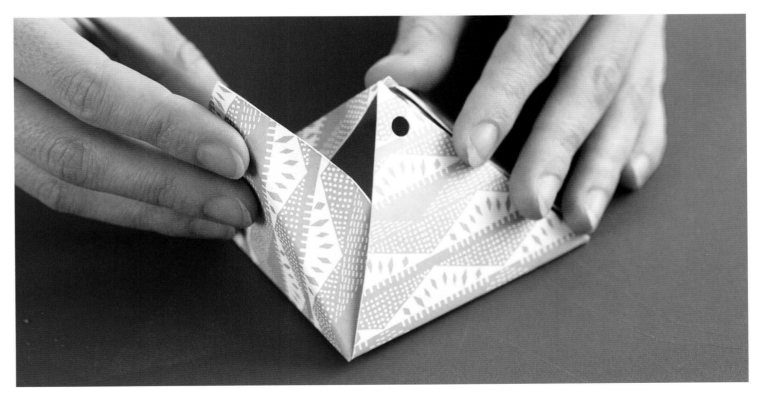

6 Assemble the pyramid box by folding in each side and tucking each flap into the center of the box. Fasten the box by threading a ribbon through the holes and tying a knot or bow.

Wirework techniques

Wire comes in many types. If you are a beginner, copper wire is very good to work with because it is malleable. Many craft stores stock wire in a range of colored finishes, and coat hanger wire is ideal when a strong structure is required. Household pliers can be used for wirework, but the serrated jaws can mark soft metals such as copper or aluminum.

Straightening a wire hanger

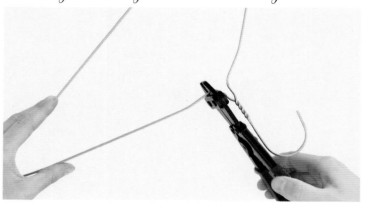

1 Cut the hanging loop and twisted section from the wire coat hanger using small bolt cutters.

2 Straighten the length you are left with—it may help to use locking pliers to straighten the corners.

Straightening lengths of wire

Pulling soft metal wire such as copper or aluminum to straighten it works well. Attach one end to a strong fixing point (a door handle for instance) and hold the other end in locking pliers. Pull until the wire is straight.

Binding wire together

To bind two lengths of coat hanger wire together, overlap the ends by at least 2 in (5 cm) and wrap medium-gauge wire around the overlap until the ends are held firmly together.

Shaping wire

Gentle curves can be bent by hand, but for tighter curves in heavy-gauge wire, use a pair of ring-bending pliers—their smooth jaws do not mark the wire. If you're following a template, have it nearby for reference.

Twisting wires

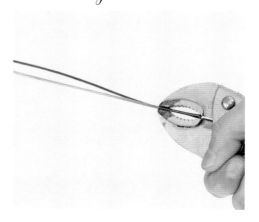

1 If you need a long length of twisted wire, bend a length of wire in half, attach it to a strong fixing point (a door handle works well) and lock the two ends in a pair of locking pliers.

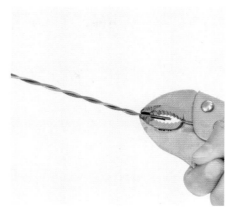

2 Pull the wire taut and turn the locking pliers until you have an even twist along the whole length. Cut the wire to remove it from the fixing point.

Joining wires

If you're working with wire and it breaks or runs out, attach another length by making a tiny loop in the end of each wire using round-nose pliers. Link the loops together, and press them closed with locking pliers.

Wrapping wire

Cut a length of medium-gauge wire one and a half times the length of the main wire. Curl the end of the medium wire around one end of the main wire, then wrap it around the main wire. Maintain tension so it is wrapped tightly and keep the spacing even.

Making a circular base

Bend a length of wire to form a circle. Overlap the ends by 1½ in (4 cm). Wrap a short length of medium-gauge wire around the overlap to hold the structure together.

Making a hanging jar

1 Cut a length of medium-gauge wire about 21½ in (55 cm) long and wrap it once around the jar, just below the lip. Twist the end around the wire to secure.

2 Pull the free end of the wire over to form a handle, then thread it under the loop around the jar. Twist the end to secure it onto the ring. Trim any excess wire.

Making an "S" hook

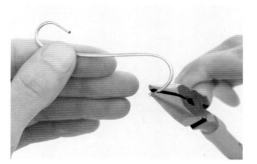

To make an S-shaped hook, curl one end of a 4 in (10 cm) piece of coat hanger wire using pliers to create a curve and the other end inward to create a small loop.

Wire heart decoration

This wire heart makes a perfect Mother's Day gift or a gift for a close friend. It's fashioned from a wire coat hanger and a handful of mother-of-pearl buttons. If you can't find any suitable buttons, use beads instead.

Materials

- wire coat hanger
- mother-of-pearl buttons

Equipment

- small bolt cutters
- mole grips
- ring-bending pliers
- fine 0.4 mm silver-plated wire
- wire cutters
- superglue

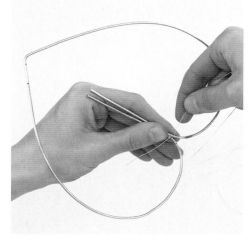

1 Cut the hanging loop off the hanger and straighten the hanger. Bend it into a heart shape, using your hands and ring-bending pliers. Cut a 8 ft 2 in (2.5 m) length of fine wire with wire cutters. At the top of the heart, where the curves meet, join the ends of the coat hanger wire with four of five turns of fine wire. Pull the wire tight, leaving a 2 in (5 cm) tail. Add a drop of superglue to fix the wire in position and leave to dry.

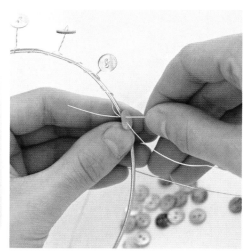

2 With the long end of the fine wire, make two loose turns along about ¾ in (2 cm) of the heart, then pull the end of the wire up through one hole in a button and back down through the other hole. Take care not to kink the wire as you pull it through

3 Hold the button ⅝ in (1.5 cm) from the heart and grip the two pieces of fine wire where they meet the heart. Rotate the button to twist the wire. Make two more turns of the fine wire around the heart, add another button, then repeat all the way round.

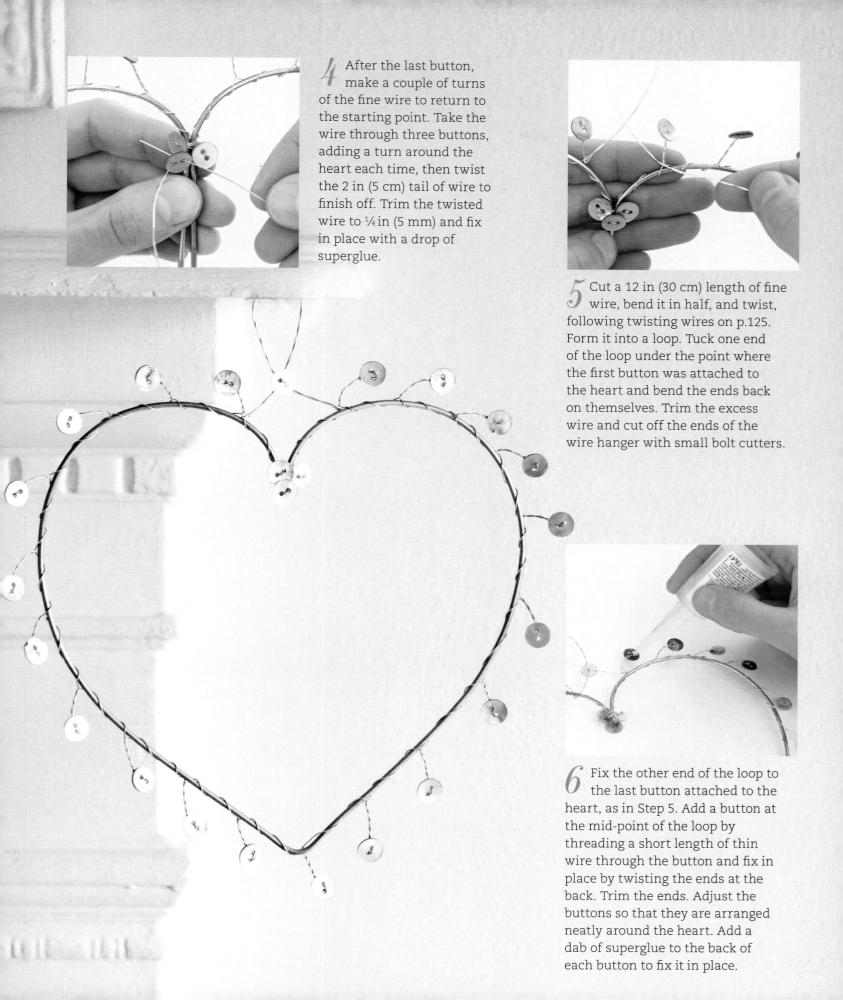

4 After the last button, make a couple of turns of the fine wire to return to the starting point. Take the wire through three buttons, adding a turn around the heart each time, then twist the 2 in (5 cm) tail of wire to finish off. Trim the twisted wire to ¼ in (5 mm) and fix in place with a drop of superglue.

5 Cut a 12 in (30 cm) length of fine wire, bend it in half, and twist, following twisting wires on p.125. Form it into a loop. Tuck one end of the loop under the point where the first button was attached to the heart and bend the ends back on themselves. Trim the excess wire and cut off the ends of the wire hanger with small bolt cutters.

6 Fix the other end of the loop to the last button attached to the heart, as in Step 5. Add a button at the mid-point of the loop by threading a short length of thin wire through the button and fix in place by twisting the ends at the back. Trim the ends. Adjust the buttons so that they are arranged neatly around the heart. Add a dab of superglue to the back of each button to fix it in place.

Wire chandelier

It's amazing to think that a few wire coat hangers and glass jars can be transformed into something so spectacular! Wrapped wire hangers form a stable structure for this chandelier, while the curled ends add a touch of elegance. Save small glass yoghurt or baby food jars and fill them with tea lights. Hang the chandelier above a dining table to create a romantic ambience.

Materials

- 10 wire coat hangers
- small bolt cutters
- mole grips
- medium-gauge wire
- wire cutters
- long-nose pliers
- 8 small glass yoghurt or baby food jars with a lip
- 8 tea lights
- wire or ribbon

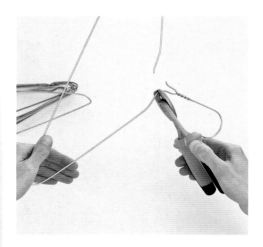

1 Cut off the hanging loops and straighten all 10 hangers, following straightening a wire hanger on p.124. Cut lengths of medium-gauge wire one and a half times longer than the length of the straightened hangers. Wrap this wire evenly around nine of the hanger wires. These will be used to construct the frame of the chandelier, while the plain wire will be cut into lengths and used to hang the jars.

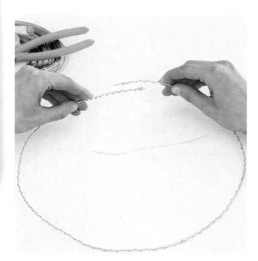

2 Use one of the wrapped wires to make a circle 11 in (27.5 cm) in diameter. This is the top tier. Overlap the ends of the wire and wrap a short length of wire around the overlap to secure.

3 Make the bottom tier by joining two lengths of wrapped wire together to make one long length, overlapping the ends by 5 in (12.5 cm). Wrap the overlap with a short length of wire. Bend the wire into a circle 14 in (36 cm) in diameter and secure the ends.

4 To make the hanging device, shape the ends of two lengths of wrapped wire into decorative curls, as shown. Wrap the other ends at opposite sides of the top tier using long-nose pliers. Cover the joins where they meet the tier by wrapping with wire. Wrap a short length of wire just below the two curls and again a little farther down to keep the two wrapped wires together.

5 To attach the pillars that link the tiers, curl a wrapped wire around the top tier using long-nose pliers, then wrap the other end around the bottom tier, 12 in (30 cm) along its length. Shape the end of the wire to create a curl. Wire-wrap the joins on both tiers and repeat to make the three other pillars, spacing them out evenly.

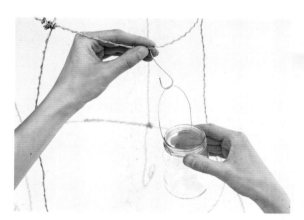

6 Make eight hanging jars, following making a hanging jar on p.125. Suspend the jars from "S" hooks made from 10 cm (4 in) lengths of the remaining non-wrapped wire. Drop a tea light in each jar and hang four jars on each tier. Finally, tie a wire or ribbon through the central stem at the top of the chandelier to hang it.

Mosaic bowl

This calming, woodland-inspired mosaic bowl is created using the direct method, meaning that tiles are glued straight onto the object and then grouted. This will not produce a completely level surface, resulting in a tactile bowl.

1 Draw a wavy line onto your bowl, about 1¾in (4.5cm) from the rim. Draw a second line ⅝in (1.5cm) below this one. This will be the first accent line on your bowl.

2 Prepare your tiles by soaking or peeling off any backing sheets. Select the plain tiles and those for the accent lines, and place them in groups of the same color and type.

3 Cut tiles for the accent lines. Wearing goggles, hold the tile between thumb and forefinger and, positioning nippers at the edge, gently squeeze. Repeat to cut into quarters.

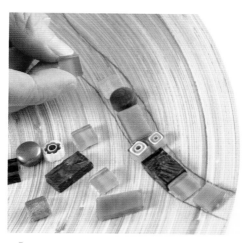

4 Arrange the tiles and embellishments between your wavy lines. Vary iridescent and matte tiles, as well as round and rectangular ones, to create a pattern.

Materials

- wooden bowl
- tesserae in different shades of green
- flat-backed beads and 5mm millefiori beads
- craft glue
- mosaic grout (either premixed or made according to the manufacturer's instructions)

Equipment

- tile nippers
- rubber gloves
- protective mask & goggles
- grout spreader
- sponge
- lint-free cloth

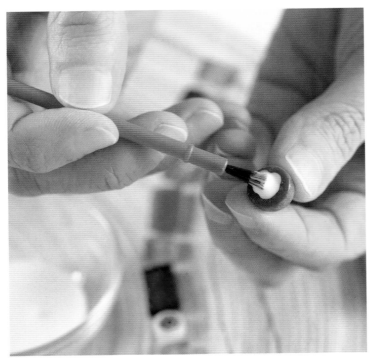 

5 Move the pieces off the line, keeping their order. Add a dab of glue to the back of each piece and stick each one to your bowl, leaving even gaps in between.

6 For the lines of plain tiles, start with the lightest green tiles and cut them in half (see Step 3). Glue them on each side of the accent line, trimming them if necessary.

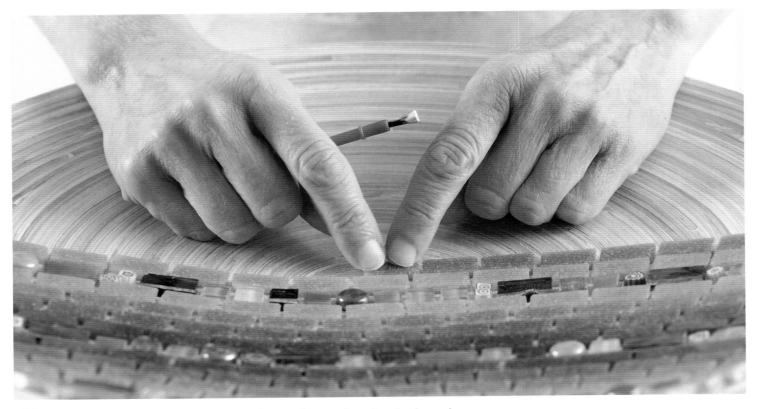

7 Complete one line at a time, increasing or decreasing the shade and adding accent lines at regular intervals. When complete, let dry overnight.

8 Wearing rubber gloves and a mask, apply the grout generously to the mosaic, working in different directions. Make sure to grout around the outer edge of the bowl, too.

9 Using a damp sponge, carefully wipe away the excess grout. Let dry for 20 minutes, then, before the grout is hard, wipe gently again.

10 When the grout is completely dry, use a lint-free dry cloth to wipe away any residue and polish the tiles to a shine.

Mosaic variations

Flower garland mirror

You will need

• Mirror with wide, flat, wooden frame

• A selection of tiles and glass pebbles

• White grout

Make this mirror in the same way as the mosaic bowl on pp.131–31. Draw on a floral design of your choice first and seal the wooden frame with watered-down craft glue if necessary. Create the flowers first, starting with a glass pebble and using tile nippers to shape the petals. Next, make the leaf garlands. Fill in the gaps with crazy paving (see above), and use tile halves to fill in the outer edge of the border. Cover the mirror with masking tape to protect it when grouting. Grout the frame, making sure to create a straight edge around the mirror.

Owl jewelry box

You will need

• Wooden box

• Glazed and unglazed ceramic tiles

• Glass pebbles and beads

• White grout

• Felt for bottom

This pretty jewellery box is made using the same technique as the mosaic bowl on pp.131–33. Start by drawing an owl design on the top of the box and then seal the box with watered-down PVA glue. Start filling in the design, attaching the nuggets and whole tiles first. Cut the remaining tiles to size to complete the design. Finally, fill in the area around the design with randomly cut tiles – a technique known as crazy paving. Allow to dry and then grout the lid. Grout the box one side at a time, waiting for each side to dry before starting the next. Glue felt to the base to finish the box.

Round tea light holder

You will need

- Ball-shaped, wooden tea light holder
- Old crockery, broken into small pieces
- Tiles and glass pebbles
- White grout
- Felt for the bottom

This tea light holder is made in the same way as the mosaic bowl (see pp.131–33), but using fragments of broken crockery. First, draw a design of your choice on the tea light holder and then seal it with watered-down craft glue. Glue down the glass pebbles first, and then use tile nippers to shape the crockery pieces into petals. Next, add any whole tiles. Finally, fill in the area around the design with more crockery pieces. Work a small area at a time. Some tiles may have to be held in place using tape until they dry. Grout, allow to dry, and attach felt to the bottom to finish.

Seaside coasters

You will need

- MDF squares
- Tiles in a variety of colors
- Gray grout

These seaside-inspired coasters have been made out of squares of MDF, using the technique described for the mosaic bowl on pp.131–33. Using your own design, first draw guidelines onto the coaster in pencil. Fill in the design first, shaping the tiles to fit. Try to keep the tiles fairly flat, since you will need to be able to rest a glass or mug on the coaster when finished. Next, fill in the background using square tiles, shaping them to fit as necessary. Again, try to keep the tiles as flat as possible. Grout the coasters, not forgetting the edges, to finish.

Fabric notebook

A brightly colored, cheery-looking notebook is always a welcome and useful gift, and if you have made it yourself it will be even more appreciated. An easy approach is to buy a ready-bound notebook and decorate the cover, but stitching and binding the paper folios together and then covering them is quite straightforward once you get the hang of it.

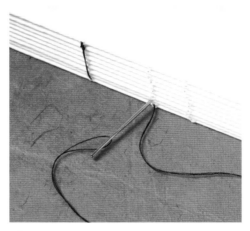

1 Align the 12 folios, with folds on the same side. Pierce 6 evenly spaced holes in each folio with a pin, then sew the folios together with running stitch.

2 Cut the piece of muslin cloth so that it is the same length and width as the joined folios. Then glue it over the stitched folio folds.

3 Glue the rectangles (the thinnest in the middle) to the fabric with a slight gap between. Glue down the fabric edges. Glue the page half over the cover.

4 Glue half of each folded paper to an inside cover and, after gluing the muslin strip to the spine, glue the other half to an outer folio paper.

Materials

- Approximately 60 sheets of letter-sized, undyed, recycled paper divided into 12 piles of 5 sheets of paper: each pile is then folded in half to make a "folio"

- 2 rectangles of recycled cardboard cut to the same size as the folded folios, and 1 rectangle cut the same size as the muslin cloth

- Old, pretty recycled fabric cut just slightly larger than a sheet of paper

- 1 illustrated page from an old, unwanted book

- 2 sheets of brightly colored recycled letter-sized paper, each folded in half

Equipment

- Linen thread and darning needle

- Strip of muslin cloth

- Eco-friendly adhesive glue

Decorated photo album

Although this decorated cover will always be delicate, it turns an ordinary-looking album into a beautiful, personalized gift. Choose a photo album or a large notebook with a neutral cloth or cardstock cover and good-quality, thick paper. Gather leaves as they start to turn rich, fall colors and look for interesting seed heads, grasses, and other natural materials.

Materials

- 1 photo album
- Variety of natural materials dried flat (p.12)
- Eco-friendly adhesive glue

Tip

Save tissue paper

Reserve any sheets of tissue paper that are wrapped around goods you buy or receive and, using an iron on a low setting, iron out the creases. Use the tissue paper to cover and protect delicate items like this album cover when not in use.

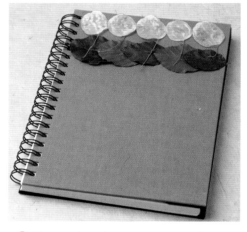

1 When your natural materials are all flattened and thoroughly dried, glue a row of seed heads or leaves along the top of the front cover.

2 For each subsequent row, glue on materials that are roughly the same size in a pattern. Overlap or alternate some materials.

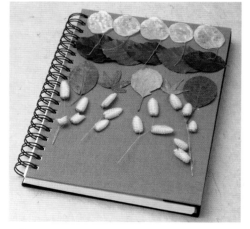

3 Continue to build up the pattern by gluing on rows of colored leaves, grasses, and twigs until the front cover is completely filled up.

4 Leave the glued materials to dry, then cover the book carefully in several layers of tissue paper before gift-wrapping it in a recycled box.

Hot-water bottle cover

This lovely winter gift is quite simple to make and will delight anyone who receives it. Collect scraps of pretty cotton material, or look in thrift or consignment shops for natural fabrics with vintage patterns and colors to make the details on this cover really unique. If you don't have an old blanket to use for the cover, use any thick, recycled soft fabric.

Materials

- Template (p.285)
- Woollen blanket or similar thick material
- 2 heart or star shapes, cut from scraps of fabric to decorate the front of the cover. Alternatively, cut 2 long strips of fabric
- 2 recycled or vintage buttons

Equipment

- Scissors
- Pins
- Cotton thread and needle or sewing machine
- Colored embroidery thread and needle for blanket stitch

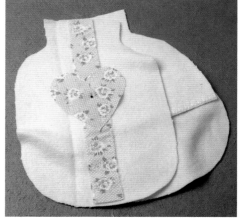

1 Using the template, cut a front panel and two back half-panels. Pin decorative shapes to the front of the cover.

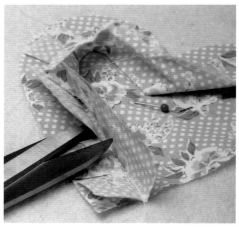

2 Sew the fabric shapes onto the front panel, leaving a seam ½ in (1 cm) wide. Snip the fabric edges every ½ in (1 cm) to make a ruffle.

3 Sew the buttons onto the fabric shape. Sew the panels together, leaving a seam of ¼ in (6 mm). The back panels should overlap slightly.

4 Using the colored embroidery thread and needle, sew all the way around the edges of the cover using blanket stitch.

Savory Christmas basket

A basket filled with homemade chutney (pp.210-13), pickled shallots, flavored oil (pp.214–15), a bag of sweet chestnuts, and a cooked ham wrapped in wax paper (pp.188–89) makes a delightful gift.

Sweet Christmas basket

Give a variety of sweet, homemade produce as a gift: package up chocolate brownies (pp.228–29), a ginger cake, mini panettone (pp.242–43), and cranberry jelly (pp.212–13) in airtight tins, pretty boxes, and decorated jars, and arrange them in a medium-sized basket.

Natural Christmas cards

If you want to post any of these homemade three-dimensional cards, choose those with the least delicate, flattest decorations and cut a piece of recycled cardstock the same size as the card. Cover the front of the decorated card with the cardstock before sealing it in an envelope. This should, hopefully, protect the decorations from disintegrating or breaking in transit.

1 Cut a piece of recycled cardstock to the correct size. Score lightly down the middle of the card in a straight line using a scalpel and ruler.

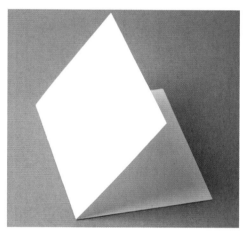

2 Fold the card in half along the scored line, which will ensure a clean fold down the center of the card.

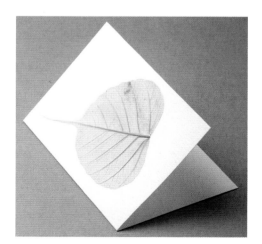

3 Arrange and stick a dried leaf onto the front of the card using small dabs of glue.

4 Glue two smaller leaves onto the larger leaf and attach one star anise at the base of the leaves. Then leave to one side to dry completely.

Materials

- Recycled cardstock
- Found objects such as seed heads, twigs, and leaves in different sizes, dried flat (p.12)
- Spices such as star anise and cinnamon sticks
- Dried ingredients such as orange slices and bay leaves

Equipment

- Scissors
- Scalpel
- Ruler
- Eco-friendly adhesive glue

Recycled paper cards

These cards are easy to make, and are a fun, child-friendly project. Tear out pages from old magazines with interesting patterns, illustrations, and festive photographs, or recycle wrapping paper, wallpaper samples, or the pictures from last year's Christmas cards. Use a selection of templates from the back of the book to cut out different shapes, or download some from the internet.

Materials

- Template (pp.278–81)
- Recycled pictures
- Plain, recycled cardstock (or find ready-made, plain recycled cards)

Equipment

- Scissors
- Scalpel
- Ruler
- Eco-friendly adhesive glue

Green tip

Recycle your old cards
Converting timber into paper is a very energy-intensive process. Recycling all cards after Christmas will save tens of thousands of tons of greenhouse gases each year.

1 Draw a template of your choice and cut it out. If you are using a star template, make up the smallest star template as well.

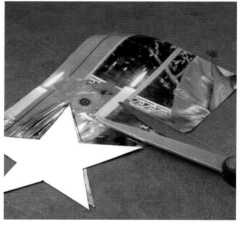

2 Place the template on a piece of illustrated or patterned recycled paper. Draw around the template and cut out the shape.

3 Lightly score down the middle of the recycled cardstock with a scalpel and ruler. Fold the card in half and glue the star shape onto the front.

4 Using the smallest star template, cut tiny stars from the recycled paper and glue them onto the card around the main star. Allow to dry.

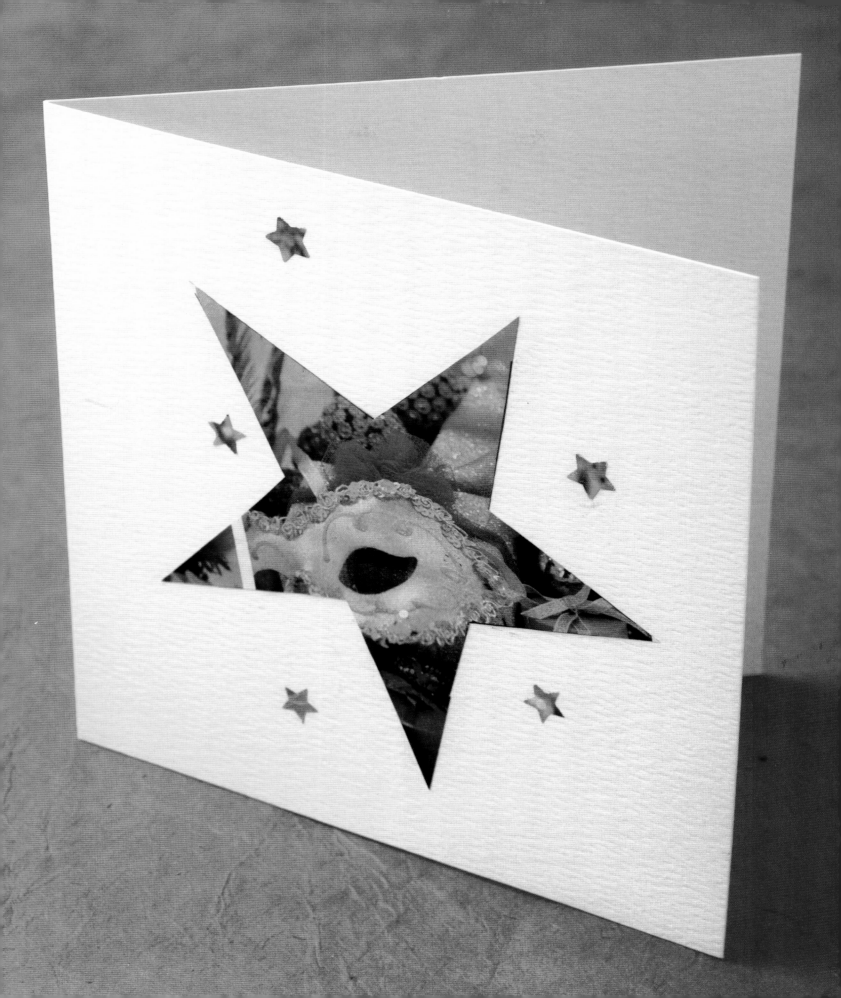

Fabric Christmas cards

These attractive cards can be easily adapted: use a loop of ribbon instead of string, or punch two small holes close together near the top of the card, thread through wool or twine, and tie it in a bow; or cut out and sew together two fabric shapes and fill the center with sweet-smelling dried lavender. Don't cut the shapes too small, or you may find them hard to sew and turn inside out.

1 Make up your chosen template, then place it on a piece of fabric and cut around the shape neatly with a pair of scissors.

2 Thread the string through the button or bead and secure the ends of the string in a knot.

3 Glue the knotted end of the string loop onto the back of the fabric shape and allow to dry.

4 Lightly score down the middle of the cardstock with a scalpel and ruler. Glue the fabric shape onto the front of the card. Allow to dry.

Materials

- Template (pp.278-81)
- Scraps of fabric, or old carpet samples, for an interesting texture
- Recycled string
- Recycled or vintage button or bead
- Recycled cardstock

Equipment

- Scissors
- Eco-friendly adhesive glue
- Scalpel
- Ruler

Square gift box

A gift box is the ideal way to present awkwardly shaped gifts. You can make this gift box exactly the required size by resizing the template. Use patterned card stock, or glue decorative paper to card stock before you create different looks.

Materials

- patterned card (or patterned paper glued onto card)
- tracing paper
- glue stick

Equipment

- pencil
- craft knife
- cutting mat
- ruler
- blunt knife (or pair of scissors)
- eraser

1 Use a photocopier to resize the box stencil on p.289. Using tracing paper and a pencil, transfer the template onto patterned card stock (or glue patterned paper to the back of the card stock).

2 Use a craft knife and cutting mat to cut out the shape you have drawn. Make sure not to cut into the internal folding lines.

3 Once you have cut out the entire shape, score all the folding lines using a ruler and blunt knife, or one side of a pair of scissors. This will make the box easier to assemble.

4 Fold the sides inward along the scored lines, making sure that each crease is sharp. For a neat finish, erase the pencil lines along the creases inside the box.

5 Attach the three sides not adjacent to the lid to each other using the glue stick or double-sided tape on the outside of the flaps. Hold in place until set.

6 Fold in the flaps of the last remaining side, spread glue or attach tape to the patterned side of the flaps, and slot the side into place. Press the flaps down and hold in place until set.

Decorating gift boxes

A few odds and ends (colored paper, ribbons, tissue paper, and buttons) can turn plain wrapped packages or dull boxes into beautiful, personalized gifts.

A. Gift tag and ribbon

Cut a luggage-label shape from white card stock. Punch a hole in the corner and thread through with ribbon. Tie this ribbon around the box and glue the ends at the base of the box. Tie another ribbon in a different color around the box.

B. Lots of dots

Layer sheets of tissue paper in different colors. Cut circles out of the sheets of tissue paper, cutting through all the layers. Using a needle and thread, sew a few small stitches through the center of each stack of circles to secure them and tie off at the back. Glue these to the box top.

C. Button bow

Cut out four rectangles in two colors of patterned card stock. Cut a triangle out of one end of each. Glue to the top of the box, layered on top of one another. Cut out a bow-tie shape from patterned card stock. Fold the sides of the bow-tie shape around and under to meet at the back. Glue this to the box and press down and glue in the middle to make the 3-D bow shape. Glue a button to the center of the bow.

D. Button band

Cut out a strip of patterned card stock long enough to wrap around the box. Sew on a variety of buttons using cream yarn. Wrap the strip around the box and glue at the bottom.

E. Floral wrap

Wrap a length of ribbon around the box and glue at the bottom. Cut out and glue another ribbon going the other way. Cut out flower shapes in different colors from tissue paper and layer on top of each other. Sew a few stitches to hold the flowers together. Glue the flowers on the box where the ribbons meet. Add a few extra smaller flowers, making them according to the same method.

F. Rosette

Cut two lengths of ribbon and point the ends by cutting out a triangle. Glue these to the top of the box. Using pinking shears, cut circles from patterned card stock and decorative papers. Cut each circle smaller as you go and stack them up to make the rossette shape. Thread a button through the circles to hold them together, then glue them on the box.

Recycled gift wrapping

Part of the pleasure of being given an imaginatively wrapped, beautifully presented gift is guessing just what might be underneath all the wrapping. If your gift is an unusual shape, put it in a discarded box first and then take the trouble to wrap the gift carefully, so that the recycled materials you choose will look their best.

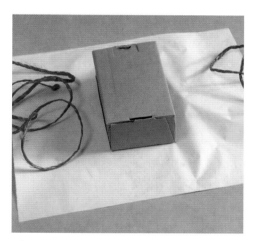

1 Put the gift in the box; shapes with flat, angular sides are easier to wrap neatly. Place the box in the center of the paper.

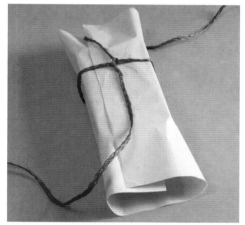

2 Fold two sides of the paper over the box so they overlap. Wrap the string around the box and tie it in a knot to hold the folded paper in place.

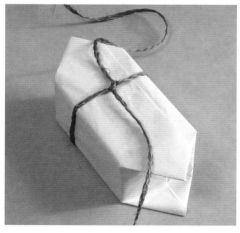

3 Fold the paper carefully at each end of the box: press the paper neatly in toward the center to create two triangular flaps at either end.

4 Fold down the flaps so they overlap. Wrap the string over the flaps to hold them in place, turn the box over, and secure the string in a bow.

Materials

• Recycled cardboard box large enough to hold the gift (optional)

• Clean sheet of recycled paper, ironed on a low setting to get rid of creases

• Colored string or ribbon (iron the ribbon on a low setting, or run through heated hair straighteners, to get rid of any creases)

Green tip

Avoid using tape
Paper can't be reused if it is covered in tape, so use ribbon, twine, upholstery trimmings, raffia, wool, or string instead. Use paper-based, water-activated gummed tape to mail a gift; duct tape has a negative impact on the environment.

Gift wrapping variations

Dish towel and vintage tartan ribbon Use a colorful dish towel and ribbon—the dish towel could even form part of the gift.

Brown paper and woven string Use recycled brown paper and make an attractive ribbon by weaving together lengths of string.

Newspaper and garden string Sheets of newspaper are a simple option, but look stylish. Tie with green string for a festive look.

Tissue paper and leaves Arrange leaves between sheets of recycled tissue paper. Secure the wrapping with glue and string.

Printed paper Tear pages from an old atlas, a map of a well-loved area, or a color magazine to make this unusual wrapping.

Paper and corrugated cardboard Over-wrap recycled paper with ridged cardboard for textural interest. Secure with a ribbon.

Vintage fabric and string Use trimmed oddments of beautiful fabric to wrap gifts. Tie simply with festively colored string.

Recycled shirt Cut the back off an old shirt and wrap the shirt front around the gift. Secure the sleeves on top with string.

Decorate gifts

Sometimes the smallest touches make all the difference, and a pile of packages under the tree can look so much more enticing if they are thoughtfully decorated. Be creative by choosing natural and recycled everyday items and trimmings instead of the usual ready-made, bought alternatives to make your wrapped gifts look special.

Create a gift basket

A recycled basket, or one made of willow or wicker from sustainable sources, makes an ideal basket.

Line the hamper with plenty of natural material like hay or straw.

Decorate jars and bottles of home-made produce with vintage fabric and ribbon.

Fill small linen sacks with nuts, fresh herbs, or cookies.

Arrange the produce on the hay so that all the labels are clearly visible.

Cut a few lengths of holly or mistletoe and tuck them inside the rim of the basket around the gifts.

Recycled and vintage items

Save brightly colored ribbon from your own gifts and purchases, or look out for vintage ribbon, iron it with a cool iron or pull it through a pair of heated hair straighteners, and tie it around gifts wrapped in brown paper. If you have a few old beads and buttons, sew or glue them onto the ribbon to create a charming, detailed effect, or thread them onto string or twine and secure the ends in a knot.

Natural raffia

Raffia is made from mulberry tree bark, which regenerates, so no trees are cut down to produce it. Gather a few lengths of raffia together, or braid them, wrap them around a gift, and tie them in an extravagant bow.

Found materials

Collect attractive natural materials and fresh foliage: pine cones, holly leaves, trailing ivy, sprigs of bright berries, dried leaves (p.12), sliced dried fruit, and cinnamon sticks all make lovely and unique final touches when tied on top of gifts.

Gift tags

Cut festive motifs from recycled patterned paper, felt, or fabric and stick or sew them onto luggage labels or small pieces of card to make gift tags; they will look much more striking than bought labels. Alternatively, stick on dried star anise and cardamom pods in simple patterns for delightfully aromatic gift tags.

Decorated gift variations

Cinnamon sticks and braided raffia Tie the gift with braided raffia, thread ribbon under it, and tie around cinnamon sticks.

Evergreen foliage and string Gather a few lengths of string, tie up the gift, and tuck a couple of sprigs of foliage under the bow.

Pine cones and raffia Tie the gift with raffia, wrap a little thin wire around the base of each cone, and tie them to the bow.

Dried fruits and raffia Glue three dried orange slices together in an overlapped row, tie the gift with raffia, and glue on the slices.

Raffia and dried leaves Gather a few lengths of raffia, tie the gift, and glue on a few dried, flattened leaves just under the bow.

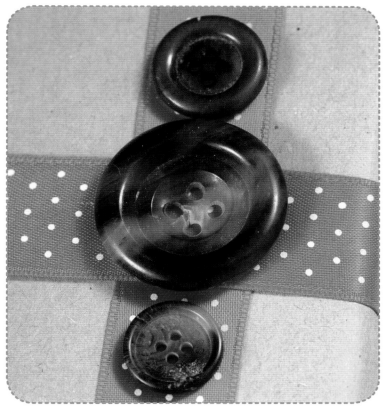

Ribbons and buttons Wrap recycled ribbon around the gift and glue different-sized buttons onto the ribbon.

Holly sprig and vintage ribbon Tie the gift with bright vintage ribbon and tuck a holly sprig with a few berries under the bow.

Threaded buttons Thread odd buttons onto a very thin length of ribbon and tie the ribbon around the gift.

Gift label variations

Dried leaf star label Glue a dried, flattened leaf (p.12) onto recycled cardboard, cut a star shape, and glue a nut in the center.

Fabric star label Glue some cheery fabric onto recycled card, cut into a star shape, and glue on a dried bay leaf and old button.

Mini star gift tag Cut out a fabric star, glue it onto folded cardboard, and decorate with a button and a little raffia loop.

Rustic bead label Push both ends of a length of garden string through a hole, thread beads onto each end, and tie in a knot.

Skeleton leaf label Thread a piece of string through the hole of a label and glue a couple of dried, flattened leaves over the hole.

Paper dove label Cut a dove template from recycled cardboard, glue on festive-looking recycled paper, and cut it out.

Paper holly leaf label Cut a holly leaf shape out of recycled paper, glue onto recycled cardboard, and add a button.

Fresh holly leaf label Sew a holly leaf onto a luggage label with festive-colored embroidery thread using simple running stitch.

3

Dinner
and
Dessert

Roasting chestnuts

To roast a handful of chestnuts over an open fire, choose a cast-iron pan, or buy a special roasting pan that has holes punched into the base. Use a sharp knife to make a small incision at the tip of each nut, and roast over a medium flame for about 15 minutes.

Spiced nuts

These coated nuts make a crunchy, very tasty homemade snack that is a tasty change from ordinary nuts and chips. If you prefer, you can substitute the spices for either cumin seeds, sesame seeds, nigella seeds, or a few chili flakes. Store any leftover nuts in an airtight jar and consume them within three days.

1 Remove all the shells, if you have bought unshelled nuts, and finely chop the rosemary leaves (discard the tough stalks).

2 Melt the butter and sugar in a large, heavy saucepan or frying pan on a low heat. Add the chopped rosemary, cayenne pepper, paprika, and salt and then toss in the nuts.

3 Stir until the nuts are evenly coated with the spice mix. Toast on a low heat, stirring or tossing frequently until the coated nuts look golden brown and crisp.

4 Tip the nuts onto a large sheet of wax paper, arrange in a single layer, and leave to cool before placing in small bowls. Serve alongside root chips (pp.176–177).

Ingredients

serves 6–8

- 10½ oz (300 g) mixed unsalted nuts
- A few sprigs of fresh rosemary
- 3 tbsp unsalted butter
- 2 tbsp soft dark brown sugar
- ½ tsp cayenne pepper
- 2 tsp mild Spanish paprika
- A good pinch of sea salt

Oven-dried root and fruit chips

These are very pretty, and you can use them as a party snack or garnish. For an extra kick, try sprinkling them with smoked sweet paprika.

1 Preheat oven to 350°F (180°C).

2 Use either the slicing attachment on a food processor, a mandoline, or a Japanese vegetable slicer to slice the unpeeled sweet potato, beet, parsnip, apple, and pear ⅛ in (⅓ cm) thick. Place the slices in a single layer on oiled baking sheets. Put into the oven.

3 Reduce oven temperature to 250°F (120°C). Bake for 1½ hours, turning the slices over every 20 minutes, until dried. Cool in single layers on wire racks. Sprinkle with salt. Serve at room temperature, with or without dips.

Get ahead
Make up to 1 day in advance. Store in an airtight container at room temperature.

Ingredients

Makes about 3 cups

- 1 small sweet potato, unpeeled
- 1 small beet, unpeeled
- 1 small parsnip, unpeeled
- 1 apple, unpeeled
- 1 pear, unpeeled
- 2 tsp salt

Equipment

- either a food processor with a slicing attachment, a mandoline, or a Japanese vegetable slicer

Quail egg and crispy bacon croustades

These attractive croustades are perfect for any special occasion. To save time, cook the eggs two days ahead and then assemble on the day.

1 Cook the quail eggs in a pot of boiling water for 2½ minutes. Drain and refresh in cold water. Peel and cut in half.

2 Spoon the mayonnaise into the croustades. Place half a quail egg on an angle, cut side up, on top of the mayonnaise. Top with the sliced bacon and garnish with the snipped chives or chervil. Serve at room temperature.

Get ahead
Cook and peel the eggs up to 2 days in advance. Cover with water and refrigerate. Fill the croustades up to 45 minutes before serving.

Variation
As an alternative filling, try with mayonnaise, black and red lumpfish caviar, and chervil or parsley sprigs.

Ingredients

Makes 20

- 10 quail eggs
- 6 tbsp mayonnaise
- 20 croustades
- 6 strips crispy bacon, sliced
- snipped chives or chervil to garnish

Butternut squash soup

Make this rich, velvety soup more
sophisticated with a garnish of sage leaves,
quickly fried in light oil.

Ingredients

Serves 4–6

- 3 tbsp olive oil
- 1 onion, chopped
- 1 leek, white part only, chopped
- 1 celery stalk, chopped
- 1lb 2oz (500g) butternut squash, peeled and cut into 1in (3cm) cubes
- 2½ cups vegetable or chicken stock
- ½ tbsp chopped sage leaves
- salt and freshly ground black pepper

Equipment

- blender or hand-held blender

1 Heat the oil in a large, heavy-bottomed saucepan with a lid. Add the onion, leek, and celery and cook for 5 minutes until they soften, but do not brown.

2 Add the squash, stock, and sage, and season well.

3 Bring to a boil, then reduce to a gentle simmer, cover, and cook for 15 minutes until the squash is tender.

4 Blend the soup, either in a blender or using a hand-held blender, until completely smooth. Check the seasoning and serve.

5 Finally, add the cymbidium orchids – they are quite dominant in this design, so it's worth arranging them last to work out where they sit best.

Variation

This soup can also be made with sweet potato or pumpkin, although the cooking times for those vegetables will be slightly less; try cooking for just 10 minutes in step 3.

Mushroom soup

Using a selection of both wild and cultivated mushrooms produces a soup bursting with flavor. The horseradish cream provides a welcome kick.

1 Melt the butter in a large saucepan, add the onion, celery, and garlic, and cook for 3–4 minutes, or until softened.

2 Stir in the mushrooms and continue to cook for another 5–6 minutes. Add the potatoes and the stock, and bring to a boil. Reduce the heat and let simmer gently for 30 minutes.

3 Using a blender, process the soup until smooth, working in batches if necessary. Sprinkle the parsley over the top and season to taste with salt and pepper. Serve immediately, stirring a little horseradish cream into each soup bowl, if desired, for an extra kick.

Ingredients

Serves 4

- 2 tbsp butter
- 1 onion, finely chopped
- 2 celery ribs, finely chopped
- 1 garlic clove, crushed
- 1lb (450g) mixed mushrooms, coarsely chopped
- 7oz (200g) potatoes, peeled and cubed
- 1 quart (1 liter) vegetable stock
- 2 tbsp finely chopped fresh parsley
- salt and freshly ground black pepper
- horseradish cream, to serve (optional)

Pumpkin and apple soup

You can cook the apples—skin, core, and all—as you will be sieving the end result. For special occasions, use dry sherry or white wine instead of water.

Ingredients

Serves 6

- 4 tbsp unsalted butter
- 1 medium onion, finely chopped
- 7oz (200g) pumpkin flesh, diced
- 2 sharp-tasting apples such as Granny Smith, diced
- 1/2 cup hot water
- 4 cups cold vegetable stock or chicken stock
- salt and freshly ground black pepper
- 2 tsp toasted pumpkin seeds, to garnish

1 Melt the butter in a large saucepan, add the onion, and cook very gently, stirring often, for 10 minutes or until soft. Do not let it brown. Add the pumpkin and apples and stir to coat well. Pour in the hot water, cover with a lid, and leave on a very, very low heat for 30 minutes, stirring from time to time. If the liquid evaporates, pour in a little more hot water. The vegetables and fruit should be very soft at the end of cooking.

2 Stir in the stock, then blend the soup in batches. As each batch is done, pour it into a sieve set over a clean saucepan. Press the contents through with the back of a ladle, a wooden spoon, or a pestle.

3 When all the soup has been sieved, reheat it very gently, then season to taste with salt and freshly ground black pepper. Serve garnished with the toasted pumpkin seeds.

Roast turkey

Cooked this way, the turkey will be juicy and delicious. Look for a smaller turkey as they are easier to cook correctly.

1 Preheat the oven to 325°F (160°C). Remove any giblets from inside the turkey and use them to make a stock.

2 Weigh the turkey so you can calculate its cooking time, then place it in a large roasting pan. Smear the breast with the butter, and season the bird well inside and out. Pop the thyme into the cavity.

3 Place greaseproof paper over the breast of the turkey, then cover it with a large sheet of foil, sealing it to the roasting pan so no steam will escape.

4 Roast the turkey for 15 minutes per 1lb (450g) of weight. Remove the foil for the last 30 minutes and increase the oven temperature to 400°F (200°C), so the skin can brown nicely. Remove the turkey from the oven and rest it, covered in foil, for at least 30 minutes before serving.

Variation
Try spreading the butter underneath the skin of the bird, easing the skin gently from the breast, before roasting.

Ingredients

Serves 8–10

- 8–10lb (4–5kg) turkey
- 2 tbsp butter
- salt and freshly ground black pepper
- handful of thyme sprigs

Cook's tips

To ensure a turkey is cooked through, use a meat thermometer to test the thickest part of the thigh. It should have a temperature of 160°F (71°C).

Clever with leftovers. A turkey yields a lot of meat. The cold leftover meat can be used in place of cooked cold chicken in any poultry recipe.

Honey-roast ham

Use a cured ham with the skin on; boiling the ham will loosen the skin. The skin should be removed before roasting, exposing the fat layer, which should be scored. If you serve this ham hot for one meal, use the cold meat in salads, sandwiches, and soups—it will keep well for a good seven days in the fridge.

Ingredients

- 6½ lb (3 kg) organic cured ham with the skin
- 2 sticks celery, coarsely chopped
- 2 carrots, coarsely chopped
- 1 onion, coarsely chopped
- 8 black peppercorns, 2 bay leaves, 4 sprigs thyme, a few fresh parsley stems, and 12–16 cloves all wrapped up in a sachet
- A handful of extra cloves
- 4 tbsp honey
- 1½ tbsp English mustard

1 Preheat the oven to 350°F (180°C) Place the ham, vegetables, and sachet in a pan. Cover with cold water. Bring to the boil, and then simmer for 1¾ hours. Then lift the ham on to a board and cut away the skin.

2 A smooth layer of fat should be left on the ham. Score the fat with a sharp knife, first in one direction and then in the opposite direction, to make a diamond pattern.

3 Stud the fat with cloves: place a clove at the center of each diamond shape. Transfer the ham to a metal roasting tray. Mix together the honey and mustard for the glaze.

4 Drizzle the glaze evenly over the fat. Roast in the pre-heated oven for about 45 minutes, basting with the glaze a couple of times, until the glaze is dark golden. Serve, or leave to cool.

Slow-cooked shoulder of pork with cider gravy

Shoulder of pork is an inexpensive and large cut, and roasts far better than a more traditional (but drier) unsmoked ham.

1 With a sharp knife, make criss-cross slits all over the skin of the pork, being careful not to cut through to the meat underneath. (You can ask your butcher to do this for you.) Rub the skin dry with paper towels and let the meat rest, uncovered, in the fridge for at least 4 hours, but preferably overnight. This will help the skin crisp while cooking.

2 Preheat the oven to 350°F (180°C). Place the meat skin-side up in a roasting pan, rub it with the oil, and rub salt all over the top, being sure to get inside the slits in the skin.

3 Pour the cider and stock into the roasting pan, being careful not to splash the top of the meat. Cover the skin with a piece of waxed paper (this will help to keep the skin from sticking to the foil), then cover the whole roasting pan with foil, sealing it tightly so that no steam escapes.

4 Roast the pork for 2½ hours, then remove the foil and waxed paper, increase the oven temperature to 450°F (230°C), and roast for 30–40 minutes until the skin is crisp. Remove the pork from the oven and wrap it in foil to keep it warm while you make the gravy. (It is a good idea to separate the crackling from the pork at this stage, as wrapping it in foil will soften it, so leave the crackling uncovered in the turned-off oven.)

5 To make the gravy, skim about ¼ cup of the pork fat from the top of the cooking juices into a saucepan and set it over low heat. Whisk in the flour and cook it for 2–3 minutes, whisking constantly, until it bubbles and starts to change color. Meanwhile, skim off and discard as much of the remaining fat as possible from the cooking liquid, then pour the juices into the pan a little at a time, whisking as you go, until you have a thick, rich gravy. Taste for seasoning. Bring it to a boil, reduce to a simmer, and cook for 5 minutes before serving with the pork and crackling.

Ingredients

Serves 6–8

- 1 bone-in shoulder of pork, preferably with the skin on, approx. 4½lb (2kg)
- 1 tbsp olive oil
- salt and freshly ground black pepper
- 1¼ cups cider
- ¾ cup chicken stock
- 1 tbsp all-purpose flour

Cook's tip

One of the best kitchen devices ever invented is a fat-separating measuring cup. The fat floats to the top of any liquid poured in, and you pour from a spout at the bottom of the cup. This allows you to use as much as possible of the natural juices from a roast, while leaving the fat behind.

Boeuf en croûte

Also known as Beef Wellington, this rich and luxurious dish is simple to finish off and serve; perfect for entertaining.

Ingredients

Serves 6

- 2¼ lb (1 kg) filet of beef, cut from the thick end and trimmed of fat
- salt and freshly ground black pepper
- 2 tbsp sunflower or vegetable oil
- 3 tbsp unsalted butter
- 2 shallots, finely chopped
- 1 garlic clove, crushed
- 9 oz (250 g) mixed wild mushrooms, finely chopped
- 1 tbsp brandy or Madeira
- 1 lb 2 oz (500 g) store-bought all-butter puff pastry
- 1 large egg, lightly beaten

1 Preheat the oven to 425°F (220°C). Season the meat all over with salt and pepper. Heat the oil in a large frying pan and cook the beef until browned all over. Place in a roasting pan and roast for 10 minutes. Remove and leave it to cool.

2 Melt the butter in a pan. Cook the shallots and garlic for 2–3 minutes, stirring, until softened. Add the mushrooms and cook, stirring, for 4–5 minutes until the juices evaporate. Add the brandy and let it bubble for 30 seconds. Let cool.

3 Roll out one-third of the dough to a rectangle about 2 in (5 cm) larger than the beef. Place on a baking sheet and prick with a fork.

4 Bake for 12–15 minutes until crisp. Cool, then spread one-third of the mushroom mixture in the center. Place the beef on top and spread over the remaining mushroom mixture. Roll out the remaining dough and place over the beef. Brush the egg around the edges of the raw dough, and press them down on the cooked dough base to seal.

5 Brush the egg all over the dough. Slit the top for steam to escape. Bake for 30 minutes for rare, 35 for medium-rare, or 45 for well done. If the dough starts to become too brown, cover it loosely with foil. Remove from the oven and let it stand for 10 minutes before serving. Slice with a very sharp knife.

Variation

This is undoubtedly an expensive dish for a special occasion, but to save a few pennies, substitute ordinary field mushrooms for button mushrooms. For extra flavor, add a handful of dried wild mushrooms, soaked in boiling water for 30 minutes, then drained and chopped, to the fresh mushrooms.

Roast side of salmon with cucumber and dill salad

A whole side of salmon makes a stunning, popular centerpiece at a party or buffet, and is really simple to prepare.

1 For the salad, toss the cucumber in the salt, put in a colander, and weigh down with a plate. Leave in the sink for 1 hour to remove the excess water. Rinse briefly, put it into a clean kitchen towel, and squeeze to remove excess water.

2 Preheat the oven to 425°F (220°C). Whisk the sugar and vinegar with 2 tbsp of boiling water to dissolve in a bowl. Toss in the cucumber and dill, cover, and chill for at least 30 minutes.

3 Put the salmon on a very large baking sheet and rub with the oil. Season well and roast at the top of the oven for 20–25 minutes, until cooked, but moist in the middle.

4 Serve the salmon with lemon wedges, the cucumber and dill salad, and a bowl of plain yogurt.

Clever with leftovers
Cold roast salmon is perfect to mix into fishcakes), or with mayonnaise and leftover Cucumber and dill salad (drained well first) to serve with crackers and salad leaves for a light lunch.

Ingredients

Serves 6-8

- 1 skinless and boneless side of salmon
- 1 tbsp olive oil
- salt and freshly ground black pepper
- 2 lemons, cut into wedges, to serve
- plain yogurt, to serve

For the sauce
- 2 cucumbers, very finely sliced with a food processor
- 2 tbsp coarse sea salt
- 2 tbsp granulated sugar
- $\frac{1}{4}$ cup rice wine vinegar
- handful of dill, finely chopped

Equipment

- food processor

Stuffed portobello mushroom en croûte

Chestnuts make a delicious, meaty-textured filling for mushrooms. These pies are wonderful served with new potatoes and a selection of baby vegetables.

1 Heat the oil and butter in a saucepan. Add the onion and celery and fry, stirring, for 3 minutes until softened and lightly golden. Remove from the heat, add the chestnuts, and mash with a fork. Work in the herbs, lemon zest, ketchup, breadcrumbs, and salt and pepper. Beat one of the eggs and stir into the mixture. Press into the mushrooms.

2 Preheat the oven to 400°F (200°C). Cut the pastry into quarters and cut a third off each. Roll out the thirds to rounds about ¾ in (2 cm) larger in diameter than the mushrooms. Line a baking sheet with parchment paper, lay the rounds on it, and place a stuffed mushroom in the center of each. Beat the second egg and brush the edges with it.

3 Roll out the remaining pastry to rounds about 3 in (8 cm) larger than the mushrooms. Place the pastry over and press the edges to seal. Make small indentations and flute the edges with the back of a knife, then brush all over with beaten egg and make a hole in the center of each to allow steam to escape. Make leaves out of pastry trimmings, if liked, and arrange on top. Brush with the remaining egg. Bake in the oven for 40 minutes or until puffy and golden and the mushrooms are cooked through.

4 Meanwhile, make the sauce. Heat the sunflower oil in a saucepan and add the chestnut mushrooms, finely chopped portobello mushroom stalks, and garlic. Cook, stirring, over medium heat for about 3 minutes until tender and the liquid has evaporated.

5 Add the cider and boil for 2 minutes until reduced by half. Stir in the cream, thyme, and 6 tbsp water. Simmer for 3 minutes until reduced and thickened, stirring. Season with salt and pepper. Transfer the pies to plates, garnish with parsley, and serve with the sauce.

Ingredients

Serves 4

- 1 tbsp olive oil
- knob of butter
- 1 onion, finely chopped
- 1 celery stalk, finely chopped
- 7 oz (240 g) can cooked chestnuts
- 2 tbsp chopped flat-leaf parsley
- 2 tbsp chopped thyme
- 1 tsp grated lemon zest
- 2 tbsp mushroom ketchup or Worcestershire sauce
- 1 cup whole wheat breadcrumbs
salt and freshly ground black pepper
- 2 small eggs
- 4 large portobello mushrooms, peeled and stalks reserved
- 15 oz (450 g) package puff pastry
- sprigs of parsley, to garnish

For the sauce
- 2 tbsp sunflower or vegetable oil
- 6 oz (175 g) chestnut mushrooms, finely chopped
- 1 garlic clove, crushed
- ⅔ cup dry, hard cider
- ¾ cup heavy cream
- 2 tsp chopped thyme

Cheese and onion pie

Soft and sweet slow-cooked onions make the perfect foil for
the buttery pastry and rich cheeses in this pie.

Ingredients

Serves 4–6

- 1 tbsp olive oil
- 2 tbsp butter
- 2 garlic cloves, finely chopped
- 2 red onions, finely sliced
- salt and freshly ground black pepper
- 2 lb (900 g) floury potatoes, such as Russets, peeled and cut into bite-sized chunks
- 5$\frac{1}{2}$ oz (150 g) grated mozzarella cheese
- 3$\frac{1}{2}$ oz (100 g) grated Emmental cheese
- $\frac{1}{4}$ oz (40 g) finely grated Parmesan cheese
- 2 x 7$\frac{1}{2}$ oz (215 g) sheets (8$\frac{1}{2}$ x 11 in/22 x 28 cm) store-bought puff pastry
- 1 large egg, beaten
- mixed salad, to serve

1 Preheat the oven to 400°F (200°C). Line a baking sheet with parchment paper.

2 Heat the oil and butter in a large, non-stick frying pan over medium heat and gently cook the garlic and onions for 25 minutes, stirring occasionally, until softened and just beginning to be tinged with gold. They should be sweet and not too brown. If they seem to be browning too fast, reduce the heat to its lowest setting and cover the pan, so the onions sweat.

3 Meanwhile, bring a large pan of salted water to a boil, add the potatoes, and cook for 10 minutes, or until just tender to the point of a knife. Drain.

4 Add the cooked potatoes to the frying pan and cook over medium heat for 5 minutes, turning carefully halfway through. Remove the pan from the heat, season well, and stir in the cheeses.

5 Place one of the rectangles of pastry on the lined baking sheet. Spoon the filling into the center, leaving a ¾ in (2 cm) border around the edges. Brush the edges with water. Place the second pastry sheet over the filling and gently stretch it to cover the first sheet. Press the pastry sheets firmly together to seal. Brush with the egg and, using a sharp knife, make three 1½ in (4 cm) slashes in the top crust to allow the steam to escape.

6 Place on a baking sheet and bake for 20–25 minutes, or until browned. Remove from the oven and place the sheet on a wire rack to rest for 5 minutes. Serve hot, with a mixed salad.

Variation
For alternative fillings, you can try half Russets and half sweet potatoes, or half potato and half butternut squash.

Stuffing and gravy recipes

Sage and onion stuffing balls

Ingredients

Serves 4

- butter, for greasing
- 1 tbsp olive oil
- 1 large onion, very finely chopped
- 1½ cups fresh white bread crumbs
- 2 tbsp finely chopped sage leaves
- salt and freshly ground black pepper
- 1 large egg, lightly beaten

Preheat the oven to 350°F (180°C). Butter a medium, shallow, ovenproof dish.

Heat the oil in a saucepan over medium heat, cover, and gently cook the onion for 10 minutes. Let cool.

Stir in the bread crumbs, sage, and a generous amount of seasoning. Add the egg and stir.

Using your hands, form the stuffing into 8 equal-sized balls. Place in the buttered dish and bake for 20–25 minutes.

Variation

Alternatively, cook the stuffing balls in the roasting pan around a chicken or turkey for the last 30 minutes of roasting time. To cook the stuffing inside a chicken or turkey, make as above up to the end of step 3 and then loosely stuff the neck end of the bird just before roasting.

Chestnut-cranberry stuffing

Ingredients

Serves 6

- butter, for greasing
- 4½ oz (125 g) pork sausage
- 2 cups fresh brown bread crumbs
- 1 tsp dried thyme
- finely grated zest of 1 lemon
- 1 red eating apple, unpeeled, cored, and finely chopped
- 1 oz (30 g) dried cranberries
- 7 oz (200 g) cooked, peeled chestnuts, roughly chopped
- 1 large egg, lightly beaten
- salt and freshly ground black pepper

Preheat the oven to 350°F (180°C). Butter a medium ovenproof dish.

Place all the ingredients in a medium mixing bowl, season generously, and stir well to combine.

Using your hands, form the stuffing into 18 equal-sized balls. Place into the prepared dish and bake for 20 minutes.

Variation

To cook the stuffing inside a chicken or turkey, loosely stuff the neck end of the bird just before roasting. Never stuff with a stuffing containing raw egg or meat ahead of time, as that poses a risk of food poisoning.

Herby apricot stuffing

Ingredients

Serves 4–6

- butter, for greasing
- 3½ oz (100 g) dried apricots, finely chopped
- juice of 1 orange
- 1 piece crystallized ginger, finely chopped
- 1 cup fresh white bread crumbs
- ¾ oz (20 g) toasted pine nuts
- 3 tbsp chopped flat-leaf parsley leaves
- 4 sprigs of rosemary, leaves chopped
- ¼ cup vegetable shortening vegetable suet
- 1 large egg, lightly beaten
- salt and freshly ground black pepper

Preheat the oven to 350°F (180°C). Butter a medium ovenproof dish.

Place all the ingredients in a medium mixing bowl, season generously, and stir well to combine.

Spoon the stuffing into the prepared dish and bake for 30 minutes.

Variation

If you do not have pine nuts, chopped hazelnuts, pecans, or almonds can be substituted instead.

Classic pan gravy

Ingredients

Serves 4

- pan juices from a roast
- 1 heaping tbsp all-purpose flour
- up to 1¼ cups chicken stock, if needed
- 2 tbsp sherry or marsala (optional)
- 1 tbsp redcurrant jelly
- salt and freshly ground black pepper

When the roast has cooked and is resting, pour off all the cooking juices into a bowl.

Add 3 tbsp of the fat, which floats to the top, back into the roasting pan. Place the roasting pan over low heat and add the flour. Cook the flour, whisking constantly, for 2–3 minutes until it bubbles and starts to color.

Meanwhile, skim off as much of the remaining fat as possible from the cooking liquid and discard it, then pour the juices into the flour mixture a little at a time, whisking as you go, until you have a thick, rich gravy. Use the chicken stock if you need more liquid. Add the sherry (if using) and the redcurrant jelly and taste for seasoning.

Bring it to a boil, making sure the jelly has melted, reduce to a simmer, and cook for 5 minutes before serving.

Variation

For a lighter gravy, just add a little white wine to the cooking juices (omit the flour, sherry, and jelly), and whisk over low heat until they reduce to a thinner gravy, then season to taste.

Vegetable recipes

Best roast potatoes

Ingredients

Serves 4

- 2 lb 4 oz (1 kg) white potatoes, such as Russet, peeled and halved

- sea salt

- 3 heaping tbsp goose or duck fat

Preheat the oven to 400°F (200°C). Bring the potatoes to a boil in a large pan of salted water. Reduce the heat to a brisk simmer and cook, uncovered, for 10 minutes, until softening at the edges. Drain, return to the pan, and place over low heat for a minute to remove excess water, then remove from the heat, cover, and shake to rough up the edges.

Meanwhile, put the fat in a roasting pan big enough to take the potatoes in a single layer. Heat in the oven for 5 minutes.

Carefully remove the pan from the oven and add the potatoes. Turn to coat in fat, spread out, and sprinkle generously with salt. Roast for 45 minutes to 1 hour, turning them after they form a crust underneath.

Perfect mashed potatoes

Ingredients

Serves 4–6

- 2 lb 4 oz (1 kg) floury potatoes, such as Russets, peeled and cut into large chunks

- salt and freshly ground black pepper

- $1/4$ cup whole milk or half-and-half

- 2 tbsp butter

- pinch of granulated sugar

Bring the potatoes to a boil in a large pan of cold salted water. Reduce the heat to a brisk simmer and cook, uncovered, for 20–25 minutes until soft, but not breaking up. Drain well in a colander.

Heat the milk and butter over low heat until the butter melts and the milk is hot, but not boiling. Add the sugar and season well. Return the potatoes to the pan and mash them well with a masher, or for a perfectly smooth result press them through a potato ricer.

Finally, use a wooden spoon to beat the potatoes really well. This helps make them super-smooth and fluffy.

Clever with leftovers

If you have leftover mashed potato, add any of the following in any combination for some different flavors: a handful of chopped spring onions, a handful of chopped flat-leaf parsley, 1 tbsp rinsed and chopped capers, finely grated zest of $1/2$ lemon, and a pinch of chile flakes.

Creamy cauliflower cheese

Ingredients

Serves 4

- 1 cauliflower, cut into florets
- 4 tbsp butter
- $\frac{1}{4}$ cup all-purpose flour
- 2 cups whole milk
- $3\frac{1}{2}$ oz (100 g) grated aged Cheddar cheese
- salt and freshly ground black pepper
- 1 tbsp Dijon mustard (optional)

Special equipment

- 10 in (25 cm) ovenproof dish

Steam the cauliflower for about 7 minutes until it is tender, but still firm, then drain and arrange it in a 10in (25cm) ovenproof dish, with the stems underneath and the florets fitting together. Preheat the oven to 350°F (180°C).
Meanwhile, melt the butter in a small, heavy-bottomed saucepan. Whisk in the flour over low heat and cook for 2 minutes, whisking. Take off the heat and slowly whisk in the milk until smooth.
Return to the heat and cook, stirring constantly right into the edges of the saucepan, for 5 minutes. Add $2\frac{1}{2}$ oz (75 g) of the cheese, the seasoning, and mustard (if using), and cook for 2 minutes until the cheese has melted and the sauce is creamy.
Pour the sauce over the cauliflower, scatter with the remaining cheese, and bake at the top of the oven for 15–20 minutes, or until golden brown all over.

Mashed carrots and rutabaga

Ingredients

Serves 4

- 10 oz (300 g) carrots, cut into small pieces
- 7 oz (200 g) rutabaga, cut into small pieces
- salt and freshly ground black pepper
- 2 tbsp butter
- 1 tsp light brown sugar (optional)
- pinch of grated nutmeg

Boil the vegetables together in a large pan of boiling salted water for about 20 minutes, or until soft. Drain well and return them to the pan.
Add the remaining ingredients and mash the vegetables well before serving.

Vegetable recipes

Glazed carrots with nutmeg

Ingredients

Serves 4–6

- 10 oz (300 g) thin, young carrots, peeled weight, cut into ¹/₂in (1cm) rounds
- salt and freshly ground black pepper
- 1 tbsp butter
- ¹/₂ tsp granulated sugar
- pinch of nutmeg

Cook the carrots in plenty of boiling salted water for about 7 minutes until they are really soft. Drain well.
Put the butter in the pan in which you cooked the carrots and allow it to melt over a low heat. Stir in the sugar and nutmeg and cook gently until the sugar dissolves. Return the carrots, season well, and turn them in the butter until well glazed.

Prepare ahead
If you have a large meal to prepare, cook the carrots to the end of step 1 ahead of time, cover, and refrigerate for up to 3 days. Reheat them in the melted butter glaze, following step 2, for 2–3 minutes until hot throughout.

Slow-cooked red cabbage

Ingredients

Serves 4–6

- 4 tbsp butter
- 2 tbsp granulated sugar
- 1 tsp salt
- 6 tbsp white wine vinegar
- 1 red cabbage, approx. 2 lb 4 oz (1 kg), shredded
- 2 tbsp redcurrant or sour cherry jelly
- 2 apples, peeled and grated
- salt and freshly ground black pepper

Equipment

- large Dutch oven

Preheat the oven to 325°F (160°C). Heat the butter, sugar, salt, vinegar, and 6 tbsp of water in a large Dutch oven. Bring to a boil, then reduce to a simmer and cook for just 2 minutes.
Add the red cabbage and stir it through. Seal the pan with a thick piece of foil, then put on the lid.
Cook in the center of the oven for 1¹/₂ hours. Remove the lid and stir in the jelly and apples, adding a little more water if the cabbage looks dry. Season generously, cover, and return to the oven for a final 30 minutes before serving.

Batching and freezing
This is one of the few vegetable dishes that freeze well. If you have a large red cabbage, just weigh it and increase the other ingredients accordingly. Cook it all and freeze leftovers for another meal.

Brussels sprouts with pancetta and chestnuts

Ingredients

Serves 4–6

• salt and freshly ground black pepper

• 1lb 2oz (500g) baby Brussels sprouts

• 1 tbsp butter, plus extra if needed

• 1 tbsp olive oil

• 3¹/₂oz (100g) chopped pancetta

• 3¹/₂oz (100g) cooked and peeled chestnuts, roughly chopped

Bring a large pan of salted water to a boil. Cook the Brussels sprouts for 4–5 minutes, until they are just cooked, then drain well and refresh them under cold water. Drain again and set aside.

In a wok, heat the butter and olive oil. When the butter has melted, add the pancetta and cook over medium heat for 3–4 minutes, until it is crispy. Add the chestnuts and cook for another minute.

Add the Brussels sprouts and cook for another 2–3 minutes, until heated through, adding a little more butter if necessary and seasoning well with pepper (not salt as the pancetta is quite salty).

Variation

For an Asian take on sprouts, shred the blanched sprouts. Stir-fry in 2 tbsp of oil over high heat, adding 1 finely chopped chile, 1 finely grated garlic clove, and 1 in (2.5 cm) finely grated fresh ginger. Finish with a splash each of soy sauce and rice wine.

Herby roasted roots

Ingredients

Serves 4

• 2lb 4oz (1kg) mixed root vegetables, such as waxy potatoes, carrots, parsnips, or butternut squash, cut into large wedges

• 1 large red onion, cut into wedges

• 3 tbsp olive oil

• handful of mixed herb leaves, such as parsley, sage, and thyme, finely chopped

• salt and freshly ground black pepper

Preheat the oven to 400°F (200°C). Mix all the vegetables, the oil, and herbs, and season well.

Arrange in a single layer in a large roasting pan and roast at the top of the oven for 45–55 minutes, turning occasionally, until browned at the edges and cooked through.

Pickle vegetables

If you have an abundance of fresh vegetables, pickle some of them in homemade spiced pickling vinegar to preserve them for the Christmas season, or to give away in a gift basket. The pickling process transforms the taste and texture of these fresh vegetables into more complex flavors, which taste good with a variety of different foods such as fish, game, and cold meats.

Homemade spiced pickling vinegar

Ingredients

- 6 cups (1.14 liters) malt vinegar
- A few pieces of blade mace
- 20 cloves
- 20 whole allspice berries
- 1 cinnamon stick
- 6 peppercorns
- 1 cup raw cane sugar

1. Boil all the ingredients together in a pan for a few minutes. Then cover and leave the liquid for 2 hours to cool completely. Strain into sterilized bottles until needed.

2. Use preserving jars with vinegar-proof lids when you bottle the vegetables in pickling vinegar. Leave the pickles to mature for at least three months before using them.

Salt, oil, and vinegar all prevent vegetables from decay by protecting them from the bacteria that could rot them. Salt draws out moisture and creates an inhospitable environment for bacteria, oil coats the produce to prevent contamination from the air, and the acid in vinegar, known as acetic acid, inhibits bacterial growth. Pickling combines the preservative qualities of salt and vinegar, and it's an ideal way to preserve vegetables such as beans, cabbage, cauliflower, cucumbers, onions, and shallots. Use the freshest, crispest produce for the best results.

Brining and potting up

The vegetables need "brining" in salt water first before being preserved in vinegar, to draw out the moisture that would otherwise seep into the vinegar and dilute it. The brining time varies: dense vegetables such as shallots need longer than beans or cucumbers. Use coarse salt, as it contains none of the anti-caking agents that are added to table salt. For 3$^1/4$ lb (1.5 kg) of shallots, mix 8 pints (4.5 liters) of water and 1 lb (450 g) salt into a brine, add the shallots, and leave for 12 hours with a plate on top to weigh the shallots down and keep them submerged. Then skin the shallots and cover them with fresh brine for a further 24 hours before placing them in sterilized preserving jars. Pour over the spiced pickling vinegar (left) to completely cover them, and then seal the jars. As well as preserving the vegetables, this spiced pickling vinegar adds a lovely delicate flavor.

Preserved lemons

If lemons are salted and left to cure in a jar, the rind turns into a rich, rounded flavor that adds a marvelously distinctive Middle-Eastern flavor to dishes. Chop the rind and rub it with garlic over a chicken or leg of lamb before roasting, mix it with roasted onions, garlic, and pumpkin pieces, some cooked couscous, raisins, pine nuts, and a stick of cinnamon, or add it to slow-cooked casserole dishes.

Ingredients

These quantities are approximate, but should fill a 3.5-cup (1-liter) jar; adjust the quantities accordingly

- 5 unwaxed organic lemons
- 1 lb 1½ oz (500 g) coarse sea salt
- 2 cinnamon sticks (optional)
- 1 tbsp coriander seeds (optional)
- 1 tbsp whole cumin seeds (optional)
- 1 tsp black peppercorns
- 1 tsp cloves (optional)
- 3 dried red chilies (optional)
- Dried bay leaves
- Enough freshly squeezed lemon juice to cover the contents of the jar

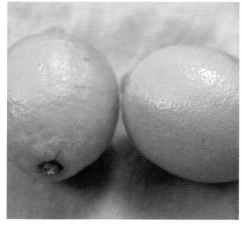

1 Sterilize the preserving jar. Wipe the lemons to remove any dirt.

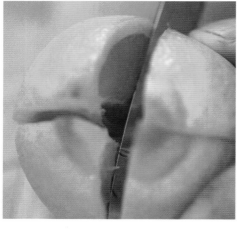

2 Cut two thirds of the way through each lemon with a sharp knife, then again at right angles to the first cut.

3 Open out the top of each lemon slightly, fill the cuts with salt, and press the top of each lemon together again. Put a couple of lemons in the jar and pack the salt in around them.

4 Fill jar with the salt, lemons, spices, and bay leaves. Cover with the lemon juice and seal. Leave for at least two months while the salt slowly dissolves to create a clear liquid.

Pear chutney

Use the largest heavy-based saucepan you have, or a preserving pan, to make chutney. As the ingredients simmer, check on them frequently and give them a stir so that they don't catch on the bottom of the pan and burn, which spoils the flavor. Then pot up the chutney in jars with vinegar-proof lids. To get a good spicy–sweet balance, leave the chutney to mature for at least three months.

1 Put all the fruit and vegetables in the pan with no added liquid and simmer gently, uncovered, until tender, stirring occasionally.

2 Wrap the peppercorns in the cheesecloth. Tie with the string to make a sachet. Then add it and the remaining ingredients to the pan.

3 Simmer the chutney, uncovered, and stir often until it thickens and takes on a dark caramel color. This will take two to three hours.

4 Remove the peppercorn sachet, pot up the chutney in warm, sterilized jars, and seal. Store in a cool, dark place.

Ingredients

Makes c. 6 lb (2.5 kg)

- 3 lb (1.4 kg) pears, peeled, cored and cut into ¾ in (2 cm) cubes
- 1 lb (450 g) onions, chopped
- 1 lb (450 g) green or red tomatoes, sliced
- 8 oz (250 g) raisins, chopped
- 6 peppercorns
- 700 g (1½ lb) brown sugar
- 1 tsp cayenne pepper
- 1 tsp ground ginger
- 2 tsp salt
- 3 cups (750 ml) malt vinegar

Equipment

- Small piece of cheesecloth
- Length of string

Cranberry jelly

This tart, fruity preserve is not only perfect with a roast turkey or chicken on Christmas day, but it also complements pork, sausages, and any cold meats you may serve over the festive season. Store the jars in a pantry or a cool, dark cabinet for up to one year. Once opened, a jar of jelly should keep well in the fridge for up to three weeks.

Ingredients

Makes about 2 cups of jelly

- 1 lb (450 g) fresh cranberries
- 1½ cups water
- 1 lb (450 g) superfine sugar

Cook's tip

Frozen cranberries

If you find it hard to find fresh cranberries, a bag of frozen fruits will work just as well for this recipe (avoid dried cranberries). There's no need to thaw the berries first before you cook them.

1 Check the cranberries and discard any that have brown spots or are shriveled. Put the berries and water in a saucepan and bring to the boil over a medium heat.

2 Turn the heat down and simmer the mixture until the cranberries are tender. Then place a fine sieve over a bowl and pour the cranberry mixture into the sieve.

3 Press the berries through the sieve with a spoon to produce a smooth pulp in the bowl. Return the pulp and juice to the saucepan, bring to the boil, and add the sugar.

4 Allow the mix to simmer for 10 minutes, then test for the setting point. If the jelly sets when tested, pour into sterilized jars, seal, label, and date the jars.

Make flavored oils

Homemade infused oils are a wonderfully instant way of adding an extra shot of flavor to your cooking, salads, and marinades. They make a perfect gift for food lovers and serious cooks alike, so bottle a selection of flavored oils and add gift labels, or include one or two in a gift basket. Good flavorings to use include fresh herbs, garlic, whole spices, pink peppercorns, or dried chilies.

Infused oils have the potential to support the growth of bacteria, so you should follow the procedures for bottling flavored oils carefully, and make sure that any ingredients you use are washed and thoroughly dried first. Use pretty recycled bottles or jars for these oils.

Sterilizing equipment

It's important to sterilize all bottles or jars and their lids before adding any ingredients. Wash them in soapy water, or put them through a hot dishwasher wash, and leave to drain until nearly dry. Then place them upside down in a cold oven and heat them for 10–15 minutes at 300°F (150°C). Leave them upturned on a clean cloth until you are ready to use them so that dust or dirt, which could contaminate the product, can't be trapped inside. Alternatively, you can boil the bottles in a large saucepan covered with water for 15 minutes, dry them thoroughly with a fresh clean cloth, and upturn them onto another cloth until they are ready to be used.

Making the oils

Make the flavored oil a week before you need it. For Rosemary oil, choose one large sprig of fresh rosemary (about 6 in/15 cm long) and bruise it with the end of a rolling pin; for Lemon oil use 3–4 large ribbons of lemon peel; for Chili oil use 3–4 whole chilies cut in half lengthwise. Put your choice of dry ingredients into a clear, sterilized glass bottle (at least 1 pint/570 ml in capacity) and add 1 pint (570 ml) of light olive oil. Make sure the dry ingredients stay below the surface of the oil, or they may turn moldy. Secure the lid firmly and shake well once a day for a week to allow the flavors to develop. Add a gift label with instructions to store the oil in the fridge and use within a week.

Wash and thoroughly dry all ingredients to be used as flavorings before putting them in a bottle and adding the oil.

Flavoured oils

Homemade flavored oils make beautiful and useful gifts for anyone who loves to cook. Herb-flavored oils can be used to dress salads or as a base for marinades, while a few drops of chili oil add zing to pizza and pasta dishes.

1 Slice the regular chiles in half with a knife, cutting all the way through the stem. Add the sliced chiles, whole bird's eye chiles, and any seeds to the sterilized bottle.

2 Fill up the bottle with 3½ cups olive oil and stopper it. The oil will keep for up to one month.

Flavoured oil variations

Basil oil

Fragrant basil oil makes a flavorful base for salad dressings, and it can be used to flavor sauces and soups. Bruising the leaves before you pour on the oil releases their delicate aroma.

Ingredients

- 13½ cups light olive oil
- 5oz (150g) basil

1 Heat the oil gently in a pan until it reaches 104°F (40°C)

2 Lightly bruise the basil and put it in a warm, sterilized jar or bottle. Pour the warm oil into the jar, then seal. The oil will be ready to use in three to four weeks.

Garlic and rosemary oil

This traditionally flavored oil can be used as a base for marinades, or to lightly coat vegetables before they are roasted in the oven. The oil keeps for one month.

Ingredients

- 6 garlic cloves
- 3 stalks rosemary
- 3½ cups light olive oil

1 Crush the garlic cloves lightly. Place them in a sterilized jar or bottle with the stalks of rosemary.

2 Add oil to the bottle to cover the herbs, then seal.

Walnut bread

To help bread cook well, mist the inside of the oven with a water spray just before baking the dough. The loaf is cooked if it sounds hollow when tapped on the base. This walnut bread will keep in a bread safe for up to four days, and it also freezes well. If you want to reheat it in a low oven, rub a little water over it beforehand to prevent it from drying out as it warms up.

Ingredients

Makes 2 ring loaves

- 3¼ cups all-purpose white bread flour
- ¾ cup dark rye flour
- 1½ tsp dried yeast
- 2 tsp salt
- 1½ cups tepid water
- 2 cups walnuts, crushed

Cook's tip

Kneading bread
The action of kneading warms and stretches the gluten in flour. This elasticity, and the action of yeast, gives bread its light, springy texture. Press and stretch the dough away from you, then lift the edges into the middle, give it a quarter turn, and repeat.

1 Preheat the oven to 450°F (230°C). Mix the flours together, then add the yeast and salt. Add a little of the water (it should be tepid); mix the ingredients. Gradually add more water until the mixture becomes a dough.

2 Add the nuts to the dough, knead the dough for 5–8 minutes until pliable, place it in a lightly oiled bowl, cover with a damp dishcloth, and leave it to rest until it doubles in size.

3 Turn the rested dough out onto a clean, lightly floured surface again and divide it into two equal amounts. Knead each half of the dough into a tight ball.

4 Shape each ball into a ring with a hole the size of a fist. Place on a lightly floured baking sheet and cover with a damp dishcloth until they double in size. Then bake for 20–25 minutes.

Focaccia bread

This bread tastes so good that it's unlikely you'll have much left over after serving it, but it keeps well in a bread safe for two days or so. When you turn the bread out onto a wire rack to cool after baking, drizzle a little olive oil over the surface. The bread will soak up the oil as it cools to give even more flavor.

1 Preheat the oven to 375°F (190°C). Roast the bulbs, cut side down, for 20 minutes or until soft. Squeeze the cooked cloves from their skins into a small bowl. Mash lightly so that some cloves remain whole. Set aside.

2 Put the flour in a bowl and make a well in the center. Add the yeast and salt, half the water, and all the oil. Using a fork, draw the flour from the edge of the bowl into the well.

3 Stir in the rest of the water, bit by bit, until it forms a dough. Knead the dough for 5 minutes, then leave it in a clean, lightly floured, covered bowl to rest for 1 hour.

4 Knock the air out of the dough. Spread it out in a floured baking tray, rub in olive oil, scatter over garlic and rosemary, and leave to rest, covered, for 30 minutes. Then bake for 20 minutes or until the surface is golden brown.

Ingredients

- 3 whole bulbs garlic with their bases sliced off
- 1 lb 2 oz (500 g) white self-rising flour
- 1 tsp fast-action dried yeast
- 1 tsp salt
- 1¼ cups tepid water
- A good glug of olive oil—about ¼ cup
- Fresh rosemary leaves, chopped, from several rosemary sprigs

Anadama bread

This dark, sweet cornbread originally hails from New England. It is curiously sweet and savory at the same time.

Ingredients

Serves 4

- ½ cup whole milk
- ½ cup polenta or fine yellow cornmeal
- 4 tbsp unsalted butter, softened
- ½ cup blackstrap molasses
- 2 tsp dried yeast
- 2½ cups all-purpose flour, plus extra for dusting
- 1 tsp salt
- vegetable oil, for greasing
- 1 large egg, lightly beaten, for glazing

Cook's tip

Slashing the loaf allows the bread to continue rising in the oven, and so does the steam from the pan of boiling water. They also help to give the bread a good crust.

1 Heat the milk and ½ cup of water in a small saucepan. Bring to a boil and add the polenta. Cook for 1–2 minutes or until it thickens, then remove from the heat. Stir in the butter until well mixed. Beat in the molasses, then set aside to cool.

2 Dissolve the yeast in ½ cup of warm water and stir well. Sift the flour and salt into a bowl and make a well. Gradually stir in the polenta mixture, then add the yeast mixture to make a soft, sticky dough.

3 Turn the dough onto a lightly floured work surface. Knead for about 10 minutes until soft and elastic. It will remain fairly sticky, but should not stick to your hands. Knead in a little flour if it seems too wet. Put the dough in a lightly oiled bowl, cover loosely with plastic wrap, and let rise in a warm place for up to 2 hours. The dough will not double in size, but should be very soft and pliable when well-risen.

4 Turn the dough onto a lightly floured work surface and gently knock it back. Knead it briefly and shape it into a flattened oval, tucking the sides underneath the center of the dough to get a tight, even shape. Place on a large baking sheet and cover loosely with plastic wrap and a clean kitchen towel. Let it rise in a warm place for about 2 hours. The dough is ready to bake when it is tight and well risen, and a finger gently poked into the dough leaves a dent that springs back quickly.

5 Preheat the oven to 350°F (180°C). Place one oven rack in the middle of the oven and another below it, close to the bottom. Boil a pot of water. Brush the loaf with a little beaten egg and slash the top 2 or 3 times with a sharp knife on a diagonal. Dust the top with flour, if desired, and place it on the middle rack. Place a roasting pan on the bottom rack, then quickly pour the boiling water into it and shut the door.

6 Bake for 45–50 minutes until the crust is nicely darkened and the bottom sounds hollow when tapped. Remove from the oven and let cool on a wire rack. Serve with Emmental or Gruyère cheese, or buttered and topped with ham and mustard.

Vanilla cookies

The melted candies in these cookies look like tiny stained-glass windows when they catch the light. Make a mixture of some plain cookies and some with sweet centers, and if you want to hang the cookies from your tree as edible decorations, make a small hole in the top of each shape before baking them. The sweet mix is very hot as the cookies come out of the oven, so take care.

Ingredients

Makes 12 cookies

- 1 stick butter
- 1¼ cups superfine sugar
- ½ tsp vanilla extract
- 2 eggs
- 4¾ cups all-purpose flour
- 2 tsp baking powder
- 2 tsp ground cinnamon
- ½ tsp salt
- A little milk
- A handful of organic hard candies, crushed (put candies of one color in a clean, recycled plastic bag and crush them with a rolling pin)

1 Preheat the oven to 375°F (190°C). Place buttered wax paper over two large baking sheets. Cream together the butter and sugar in a large bowl. Add the vanilla extract and stir in the eggs.

2 Sift the flour, baking powder, cinnamon, and salt into a separate bowl. Add the egg mix and then the milk, a little at a time, and mix into a dough. Chill for 30 minutes.

3 Roll out the dough on a lightly floured surface until ¼ in (5 mm) thick. Cut shapes using a cutter. Use a smaller cutter to make the holes, and fill each with a few crushed sweets.

4 Bake for 10 minutes. Leave the baked cookies on the paper and transfer the paper onto a wire rack. Allow the cookies to cool completely before removing them from the paper.

Chocolate brownies

Once packaged in an airtight tin, these irresistable chocolate brownies will stay their best for up to six days. Don't overcook them or they will lose their soft, fudgy quality; look for a dull crust to form, then quickly take them out of the oven. You can make the brownies in advance, freeze them, and leave them to thaw in a tin—there will be no excess moisture.

1 Preheat the oven to 375°F (190°C). Grease and line a 12 x 9 in (30 x 23 cm) baking tray with parchment paper. Put chocolate pieces and butter cubes in a bowl.

2 Melt the chocolate and butter slowly in a double boiler: rest the bowl over a pan of gently simmering water on a low heat.

3 Dissolve the coffee granules in the water in a large bowl. Beat in the eggs, sugar, and vanilla extract. Then beat in the chocolate mixture.

4 Fold in the flour and chocolate chips. Pour the mix into the tray. Bake for 20–25 minutes, or until firm to the touch. Cut into squares once cool.

Ingredients

- 12 oz (350 g) bittersweet chocolate, broken into small pieces
- 8 oz (225 g) butter, cut into small cubes
- 2 tsp instant coffee granules
- 2 tbsp hot water
- 4 eggs
- 8 oz (225 g) superfine sugar
- 1 tsp vanilla extract
- 3 oz (75 g) self-rising flour
- 8 oz (225 g) bittersweet chocolate chips or small chunks of bittersweet chocolate

Marshmallow sweets

It's essential that you use a sugar thermometer to achieve the correct boiling point when heating the sugar solution in this recipe. The sugar syrup is extremely dangerous at this high temperature, so take care and keep children well away from the pan. The soft marshmallows keep well for three to four days if stored in an airtight tin lined with baking parchment.

Ingredients

- 2 tbsp confectioner's sugar
- 2 tbsp cornstarch
- 8 sheets leaf gelatine (1 oz/25 g)
- ½ cup hot water
- 2–3 drops organic food coloring (optional)
- 1 lb 1½ oz (500 g) granulated sugar
- 1 cup cold water
- 2 egg whites

Cook's tip

Toasting marshmallows

If children want to toast their marshmallows over an open fire, tie a fork handle securely to one end of a bamboo stick with a piece of string. Push a square of marshmallow onto the prongs of the fork and give the other end of the bamboo stick to the child to hold.

1 Lightly oil a baking tray. Mix the confectioner's sugar and cornstarch and sift a little into the baking tray to coat it. Dissolve the gelatine in the water in a small bowl.

2 Put the sugar and water in a large pan, stand a thermometer in the pan, and heat the sugar syrup to 252°F (122°C). In the meantime, whisk the egg whites until stiff.

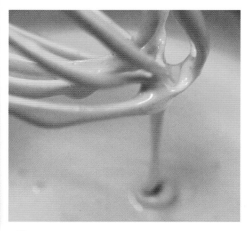

3 Take the boiling syrup off the heat and mix in the dissolved gelatine. Then gradually beat the syrup into the beaten egg whites. The texture should be thick and creamy.

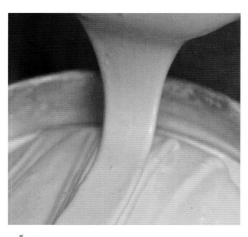

4 Pour the mix into the tray and leave to set in a cool place. Once cool, cut into squares. Lightly coat each square in the confectioner's sugar and cornstarch mix. Store in an airtight tin.

Shortbread cookies

Shortbread is traditionally baked in ceramic molds, or in a round tin and cut into petticoat tails or wedges, but use whatever shaped tray you have to hand for these crisp, yet wonderfully crumbly, cookies. To make festive shortbread shapes, roll the dough out to a thickness of ⅛–¼ in (3–5 mm), cut the shapes with cookie cutters, and bake in the oven for 12–15 minutes.

1 Preheat the oven to 300°F (150°C). Grease and flour a baking tray. Cream together butter and sugar in a bowl until the mix is pale. Sift and mix in flour and semolina, a little at a time.

2 Draw the mixture together with your fingertips to form a dough and tip it out onto a clean, lightly floured surface. Knead the dough to a smooth, uniform consistency.

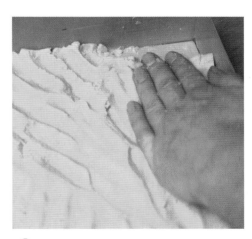

3 Put the dough into the prepared tray, press it down evenly, and prick it all over with a fork. Sprinkle sugar over the top and chill in the fridge for 15 minutes until firm.

4 Bake for 30 minutes or until pale brown in color. Leave in the tray for 5 minutes, then slice into fingers, or triangles if you have used round trays, and leave to cool on a wire rack.

Ingredients

Makes 12 cookies

- 8 oz (225 g) butter
- ½ cup superfine sugar
- 2¼ cups all-purpose flour
- ¼ cup fine semolina
- A little extra sugar

Cook's tip

Kneading and freezing
Work quickly and lightly as you knead the shortbread dough: the butter in the mix will soften and turn greasy if you overwork the dough, so the less you handle it, the better it will taste when baked. The cooked cookies can be frozen for up to one month.

Mince pies

Prepare the mincemeat ideally a week, or at the very least one day, ahead of making the pies to allow the flavors to develop. If the rolled pastry is too thick it won't cook quickly enough and the mincemeat will soak into it, turning it soggy; the right thickness results in a delicate, crispy pastry. These quantities should make 24 pies that will keep well for up to seven days in an airtight tin.

Ingredients

For the mincemeat

- 3 oz (85 g) each golden raisins, raisins, and currants
- 1½ oz (35 g) blanched almonds, finely chopped
- ½ firm apple, cored and coarsely grated
- ½ cup raw sugar
- 2 oz (50 g) candied citron, chopped
- 2½ oz (75 g) dried cranberries
- Grated zest of 1 orange
- Grated zest of 1 lemon
- 1 tsp pumpkin pie spice
- 1½ oz (40 g) lard
- 2fl oz (50 ml) brandy

For the pastry

- 2 cups all-purpose flour
- 1 stick butter, diced
- A large pinch of salt
- 1 large egg yolk
- 1–2 tbsp hot water
- 2 tbsp milk
- 1 tbsp superfine sugar

1 Mix the mincemeat ingredients in a bowl, put in a sterilized jar, and store in the fridge. For the pastry, mix flour, butter, and salt in a bowl. Add the egg and water. Form a dough.

2 Turn the dough onto a lightly floured surface and knead until smooth. Chill for 10 minutes in the fridge, then roll it out to ⅟₁₆ in (2 mm) thick and cut 24 discs with a cutter.

3 Preheat the oven to 375°F (190°C). Press each disc gently into the individual bases of a bun or pie tray. Fill each pastry case with a teaspoon of the mincemeat.

4 Top the pies with pretty shapes cut from the remaining pastry dough. Brush each with a little milk, sprinkle with superfine sugar, and bake for 18–20 minutes or until golden.

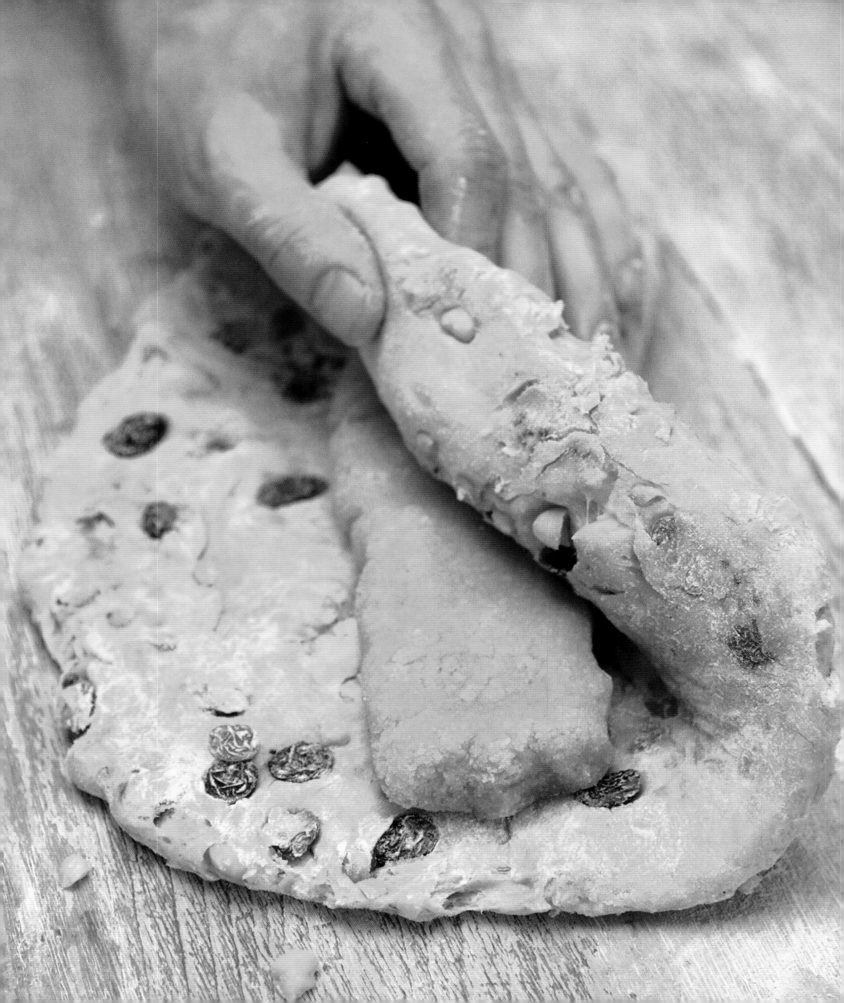

Stollen

This rich, German Christmas bread is filled with rum-soaked fruits and wrapped around an almond paste center—symbolizing the baby Jesus wrapped in swaddling clothes. The loaf is baked if it sounds hollow when tapped on the base. As you let it cool on a wire rack, brush the top with melted butter, and then dust with confectioner's sugar just before serving it.

1 Preheat the oven to 400°F (200°C). Put the golden raisins and currants in a small bowl. Warm the rum in a small pan, pour it over the fruits, and leave to one side to allow the alcohol to soak into the fruits.

2 Mix the flour, sugar, and spices, pour in the yeasty milk, and make a batter. Cover with a dry dishcloth and leave in a warm place for half an hour. Then add the butter and egg.

3 Mix into a dough, knead for 8–10 minutes, rest for 1–2 hours, or until doubled in size. Mix the filling ingredients into a paste. Knead all the fruits and nuts into the dough.

4 Roll the dough into an oval shape. Form the paste into a long roll, put it in the center, fold the dough over the paste, brush the edges with milk, rest for an hor, and bake for 30 minutes.

Ingredients

- ½ cup golden raisins
- ¼ cup currants
- 3 tbsp rum
- 3 cups white flour
- ¼ cup superfine sugar
- ½ tsp ground cardamom
- 1½ tsp ground cinnamon
- 2 tsp dried yeast mixed with ¾ cup lukewarm milk
- 4 tbsp butter, melted
- 1 egg, lightly beaten
- ¼ cup chopped candied citron
- ½ cup almonds, chopped

For the almond filling
- ¾ cup finely ground almonds
- ¼ cup superfine sugar
- 1 cup confectioner's sugar
- 1½ tsp lemon juice
- ½ egg, lightly beaten

Chocolate log

Known as a Bûche de Noel in France, this chocolate cake can be served as a dessert, or with coffee. Bake the sponge in advance if you need to prepare ahead; to keep it moist, wet some wax paper, wring it out, wrap it around the cooled sponge, and put the cake in a plastic bag. This will keep it fresh for a day or so until you are ready to roll and decorate it.

Ingredients

For the sponge
- 4 extra-large eggs at room temperature
- ½ cup superfine sugar
- ½ cup self-rising flour
- ¼ cup cocoa powder

For the filling
- 8 oz (225 g) can unsweetened chestnut purée
- 1 tbsp coffee extract
- ¼ cup superfine sugar
- ½ cup plus 2 tbsp heavy cream, stiffly whipped
- 2 tbsp brandy

For the fudge frosting
- 4 tbsp melted butter
- 3 tbsp cocoa powder
- About 3 tbsp milk
- 1 cup confectioner's sugar, sifted

1 Preheat the oven to 400°F (200°C). Grease and line a jelly roll pan. Whisk together the eggs and sugar in a large bowl until the mix is light, then sift in the flour and cocoa and fold them into the mixture.

2 Turn the mix into the prepared pan and spread it evenly. Bake in a preheated oven for 10 minutes. Turn the cake out onto wax paper and leave to cool.

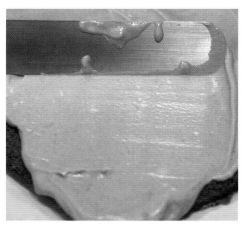

3 To make the filling, put the purée in a bowl and beat in the coffee extract and sugar until smooth. Fold in the cream and brandy. Spread the filling over the cooled sponge.

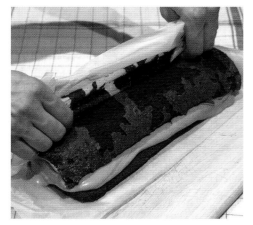

4 Peel off the paper as you roll the sponge up. Mix the butter and cocoa, add the milk and confectioner's sugar, beat until smooth. Decorate the cake to look like a log.

Mini panettone

This sweet Italian Christmas bread is rich in butter, eggs, and dried fruits, yet it is deliciously light and soft. Italians traditionally have a slice of panettone with a glass of Champagne on Christmas day. Avoid leaving any dried fruit on the surface of the dough as you put it into the molds, or it will burn in the oven and turn hard and bitter.

Ingredients

Makes 12 mini loaves

- 12 mini pudding molds, greased
- 18 oz (500 g) unbleached white bread flour
- ½ tsp salt
- 1 tsp dried yeast
- ½ cup lukewarm milk
- 2 eggs
- 2 egg yolks
- 10 tbsp butter, softened
- ¼ cup plus 2 tbsp superfine sugar
- ¼ cup mixed candied citron
- ½ cup raisins
- Melted butter for brushing

1 Preheat the oven to 180°C (350°F). Sift the flour into a bowl, add the salt, and make a well. Whisk the yeast, milk, and eggs together, pour into the well, mix in a little flour to make a batter, and rest for 30 minutes.

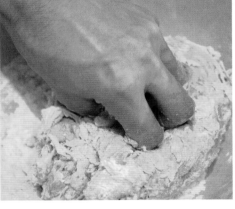

2 Add the egg yolks, softened butter, and sugar and mix them and the rest of the flour into the batter with a fork. Then bind the ingredients together into a ball with your hands.

3 Knead the dough for 5 minutes and leave to rest in a warm, but not too warm, place for 1½–2 hours, or until doubled in size. Then scatter over the peel and raisins.

4 Gently knead in the peel and the raisins. Divide into 12, place in the molds, cover with a dry dishcloth, and rest for 1 hour. Then brush the tops with melted butter and bake for 20 minutes.

Plum pudding

Early November is an ideal time to make a plum pudding, as its flavor matures and improves with age. Plum puddings are traditionally set alight before being served: heat a saucepan, add two tablespoons of brandy, immediately light the brandy with a match, pour it over the pudding, and serve.

1 Sift the flour and spices into a large bowl. Add all the remaining dry ingredients and the apple and carrot, and mix well.

2 Mix the eggs into the mixture, one at a time, then add the orange juice and rind and stir well.

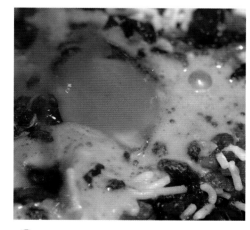

3 Add the stout, ale, or milk and mix thoroughly. Cut three circles of wax paper that will fit inside the rims of the pudding basins, then butter the insides of the basins.

4 Decant the mix into the basins, packing it down. Cover with the paper and some tin foil, and secure with string tied into a handle. Steam for eight hours, or in stages of four two hours.

Ingredients

- 1 cup self-rising flour
- 1 tsp grated nutmeg
- 1½ tsp pumpkin pie spice
- 1 tsp ground cinnamon
- 6 packed cups fresh white breadcrumbs
- 10 oz (280 g) lard
- ½ cup dark brown sugar
- 1 lb (450 g) currants
- 2 lb (900 g) raisins
- 1 lb (450 g) golden raisins
- ½ cup candied citron
- ½ cup sliced almonds
- 1 large cooking apple, grated
- 1 carrot, grated
- 6 eggs
- Juice and zest of 1 orange
- 2 cups stout, ale, or milk
- A little brandy for lighting the pudding

Equipment

- Wax paper
- Three pudding basins
- Length of string

Pumpkin pie

This is a delicate version of the classic dessert, with warm tones of cinnamon and pumpkin pie spice.

1 To make the dough, rub together the flour and butter, or pulse-blend in a food processor, to form fine crumbs. Stir in the sugar. Beat together the egg yolk and vanilla. Mix into the dry ingredients to form a soft dough, adding a little water if needed. Wrap in plastic wrap and chill for 1 hour.

2 Preheat the oven to 350°F (180°C). Roll out the dough on a floured surface to a thickness of ⅛ in (3 mm). It will be fragile, so if it starts to crumble, bring it together with your hands and knead it gently to get rid of any cracks. Use it to line a 9 in (22 cm) loose-bottomed tart pan, leaving an overlapping edge of at least ¾ in (2 cm). Prick the bottom all over with a fork. Line the crust with parchment paper and weigh it down with baking beans.

3 Place the crust on a baking sheet and blind-bake it for 20 minutes. Remove the beans and paper; if the center looks damp, or raw, which means it is uncooked, return it to the oven for 5 minutes.

4 For the filling, in a large bowl, whisk together the eggs, sugar, spices, and cream. When they are well blended, beat in the canned or puréed pumpkin to make a smooth filling. Partially pull out an oven rack from the center of the oven and place the crust on it. Pour the filling into the crust and slide the rack back into the oven.

5 Bake for 45–50 minutes until the filling is quite set, but before it begins to bubble up at the edges. Trim the dough edge with a small, sharp knife while still warm, then leave the pie to cool in its pan for at least 15 minutes before turning out. Serve warm with thick cream or vanilla ice cream.

Prepare ahead
The blind-baked, unfilled crust can be stored in an airtight container for up to 3 days, or frozen for up to 12 weeks.

Ingredients

Serves 6–8

- 1 cup all-purpose flour, plus extra for dusting
- 7 tbsp unsalted butter, chilled and cut into cubes
- ¼ cup granulated sugar
- 1 large egg yolk
- ½ tsp vanilla extract
- for the filling
- 3 large eggs
- ½ cup light brown sugar
- 1 tsp ground cinnamon
- 1 tsp pumpkin pie spice
- ¾ cup heavy cream
- 1 x 14 oz (425 g) can processed pumpkin, or 14 oz (400 g) roasted and puréed pumpkin
- thick cream or vanilla ice cream, to serve (optional)

Equipment

- food processor (optional)
- 9in (22cm) loose-bottomed tart pan
- baking beans

Gingerbread house

With its intricate piping and fondant cutout detail, this impressive gingerbread house is sure to please a crowd and provide a whimsical backdrop for your Christmas celebrations. Bake the gingerbread pieces in batches, and, once cool, use a serrated knife to refine the shapes.

Ingredients

- 1 batch gingerbread dough (see p.251)
- 1½ cups royal icing, piping consistency (see p.255)
- 3½ oz (100 g) red fondant, strengthened
- cornflour, for dusting

Equipment

- rolling pin
- gingerbread house template (see p.288)
- square, Christmas tree, heart, and circle cookie cutters
- fondant smoother
- piping bag
- round tips (such as PME no. 1, 2, and 3)
- 11 in (28 cm) white fondant-covered square cake drum
- 3 ft (1 m) red satin ribbon (½ in/1 cm wide)
- craft glue

1 Roll out the dough on a floured sheet of parchment paper, to about ¼ in (5 mm) thick. Using the template on p.288, cut out the pieces, including a spare panel. Use cutters to cut out windows and trees.

2 Transfer the gingerbread and parchment paper to a baking sheet. Bake in an oven preheated to 350°F (180°C), until golden. Cool on the baking sheet. Move to a wire rack to cool.

3 Attach a no. 2 tip to a piping bag and fill it with royal icing. Pipe tiles onto each roof panel in a series of loops. Change to a no. 1 tip, and pipe patterns and picot dots on the walls and the front of the house. Outline the windows and door, and pipe the surface of the chimney. Pipe an outline on the trees. Allow each piece to dry before assembling.

4 Assemble the house (see pp.250–51). Put the chimney together, then attach it to the house. Use the spare panel to cut a ½- in (1- cm) wide strip, as long as the roof, to run along the top. Glue to the roof top with royal icing.

5 Roll out the red fondant on a cornstarch-dusted surface and use cutters for tiny hearts, circles, and a wreath for the door. Roll small balls with your hands. Let dry overnight. When dry, use a no. 1 tip to pipe royal icing onto the wreath in dots.

6 Switch to a no. 3 tip, and decorate the seams with piped beading. Glue the fondant shapes to the house with royal icing and allow it to harden for 24 hours. Once dry, lift the house and dot the underside of the walls with royal icing. Place on the covered drum, and pipe a snail trail at the bottom. Attach the ribbon around the drum.

Building with gingerbread

The secret to a successful gingerbread construction is good-quality dough, a symmetrically drawn template, and precise baking time. You will also need patience, as you must wait for the glue or royal icing fixative to dry as you construct, to ensure a sturdy finished product.

Ingredients

- gingerbread dough (see p.251), rolled to 5mm (¼in) thick
- royal icing, for piping (see p.255)

Equipment

- cardboard or baking parchment templates

Cook's tip

Always assemble the gingerbread construction on the board on which it will be presented. Moving it later could cause pieces to shift. Colour your royal icing with colouring paste for specific shades or to make the piping stand out.

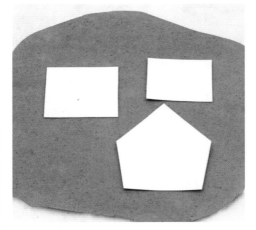

1 To create a house, lay the templates on the gingerbread dough. Use a sharp knife to cut around the templates neatly.

2 Using a palette knife, move the dough pieces onto a baking tray lined with baking parchment, ensuring they lie flat.

3 Bake according to the recipe instructions. Trim any rough edges with a sharp, hot knife, and leave the pieces to cool.

4 Once cool, pipe your designs on the cooled gingerbread pieces before you assemble your creation, if desired.

Gingerbread recipe

Firm gingerbread is ideal for creating 3-D projects with a template. Before you begin building, allow at least a week for the gingerbread to harden. Gingerbread creations are traditionally "glued" together with royal icing (see p.255) or melted, caramelized sugar (see Tip).

5 To assemble, work from the bottom upwards, applying royal icing or sugar glue (see p.255) to the joins with a palette knife.

6 Allow each join to dry. Ensure the base is dry before you attach the roof. Hold the pitched roof in place for a few minutes.

Variations

You can create trees, towers, windmills, and fairy bowers with gingerbread. For cylindrical shapes, wrap the gingerbread pieces around a can while they are warm. If you are unsure whether the construction will work, do a trial run with cardboard and glue.

1 Melt the syrup, butter, and sugar in a pan. In a bowl, sift together the flour, cinnamon, and ginger. Make a well in the center.

2 Stir in the baking soda mix, yolks, and melted syrup, sugar, and butter. Knead into a pliable dough on a flour-dusted surface.

3 While the dough is still warm, roll it out to about ¼ in (5 mm) thick. Preheat the oven to 350°F (180°C).

4 Carefully lift onto a lightly greased and lined baking sheet. Bake for 10–13 minutes, or until firm and just beginning to brown at the edges. Remove from the oven and cool on the sheet until required.

Ingredients

- ¾ cup corn syrup
- 8 tbsp butter, softened
- ½ cup brown sugar
- 4½ cups all-purpose flour, sifted, plus extra for dusting
- 1 tsp ground cinnamon
- 4 tsp ground ginger
- 4 tsp baking soda, dissolved in 4 tsp cold water
- 2 large egg yolks

Cook's tip

To make sugar "glue," melt 1 cup white granulated sugar in a heavy-bottomed pan over medium heat, until the sugar melts and browns. Be careful, since it can burn. Spread onto the gingerbread edges to glue pieces together. Beware: it is very hot.

Christmas cake

Make this cake three months in advance, store it in several layers of baking parchment in an airtight tin, and gradually soak it with brandy over a series of weeks to ensure it has a great flavor. If you don't like the taste of brandy, make the cake at least one week before you want to eat it. For a simple but elegant confectioners' sugar pattern on the cake, use a paper doily as a stencil.

Ingredients

- 1¼ cups currants
- 1 cup golden raisins
- 1 cup raisins
- ¾ cup (about 20) glacé cherries, rinsed, dried, and quartered
- Packed ¼ cup (about 14) dried apricots, cut into pieces
- ¼ cup mixed candied citrus, finely chopped
- 4fl oz (100 ml) brandy
- 2 cups all-purpose flour
- 2 tsp grated nutmeg
- 2 tsp pumpkin pie spice
- 1 cup (2 sticks) butter, melted
- 1 cup dark muscovado sugar
- ½ cup whole almonds, chopped
- 1 tbsp molasses
- Zest and juice of 1 lemon
- Zest and juice of 1 orange
- 4 extra large eggs
- Brandy for soaking

1 Preheat the oven to 275°F (140°C). Place fruits in a bowl, add brandy, and leave overnight. Grease and line a 8 in (20 cm) deep round cake pan, ensuring that the paper around the side is higher than the height of the pan.

2 Measure the flour, spices, butter, sugar, almonds, molasses, and the lemon and orange zests and juice into a large bowl and add the brandy-soaked fruits.

3 Add the eggs to the ingredients and mix everything together thoroughly. Then spoon the cake mixture into the prepared pan.

4 Spread the mix out evenly with a palette knife and cover with a double layer of wax paper. Bake in the oven for about 4½ hours until firm. Allow to cool in the pan.

Festive fruitcake

This simple yet elegant Christmas cake is covered in smooth royal icing and topped with a delicate robin run-out. Piped icicles decorate the top and a pretty fondant bow encircles the fruitcake, which can be made weeks in advance of your special celebration.

Ingredients

- confectioner's sugar, for dusting
- 1 batch marzipan (see p.258)
- 8 in (20 cm) fruitcake (see p.257)
- 3 fl oz (9 0ml) apricot glaze
- vegetable shortening
- ¾ cup royal icing, for piping (see p.255)
- red, brown, yellow, and black coloring pastes
- 1 batch royal icing
- edible pearl luster dust
- cornstarch, for dusting
- 7 oz (200 g) red fondant, strengthened)

Equipment

- fondant roller
- robin templates (see p.259)
- masking tape
- food-grade acetate sheets
- piping bags with fine piping tips (such as PME no. 1 and 2)
- turntable or lazy Susan
- offset palette knife
- 12 in (30 cm) round cake drum, iced with royal icing
- multi-ribbon cutter, straight sides
- 3 ft (1 m) white satin ribbon (½ in/1 cm wide)
- craft glue

1 Four days before you want to serve the cake, roll out the marzipan to ¼ in (7.5 mm) thick on an confectioner's-sugar dusted surface. Brush the surface of the cake with apricot glaze, and cover with marzipan. Set aside to dry for 2–3 days. Trace the robin template on a sheet of paper. Use masking tape to secure it to a flat surface. Cover with acetate and secure with masking tape. Lightly grease the surface with shortening.

2 Place half of the piping-consistency royal icing in a bowl, double-wrap with plastic wrap, and set aside. Divide the remainder into four small pots. Use coloring paste to achieve the different colors for the robin.

3 Fit a small tip (no. 1) to each piping bag, and fill each with a different color. Using the right color for each part of the robin (e.g., yellow for the beak), pipe the outline of each part of the robin. Make sure that all the lines touch each other, as shown on p.259. Keep the piping bags upright with a wet sponge around the tip, to prevent them from drying out. Make a second outline for the robin's wing on a separate sheet of acetate. Let dry for a few hours. Decant each piping bag into its own bowl and cover tightly with plastic wrap. Set aside.

4 When the outlines are hard, thin the colored icings, one by one, with some water, adding a drop at a time until it reaches the right consistency. Transfer each icing batch to a piping bag fitted with a slightly bigger tip (no. 2), and begin your run-outs (see p.259). Allow each section to dry for about 10 minutes before moving on to another color. Fill in the second robin's wing in the same way. To achieve a good shine, allow to dry in a warm, dry place for several days.

continued overleaf

Royal icing for piping

Ingredients

Makes 700g (1¹/₂lb)

• 3 large free-range pasteurized egg whites

• 1 tsp lemon juice,
plus extra if needed

• 6 cups confectioner's sugar, sifted

• coloring paste, optional

Beat the egg whites in a large bowl. Stir in the lemon juice. Gradually add the confectioner's sugar.

Continue to beat until the icing has a smooth consistency like toothpaste.

Add more lemon juice if it is too thick. Dip a toothpick into the coloring paste, if using. Add just a dot of colouring paste at a time—a little goes a long way. Mix into the royal icing and stir until you achieve a uniform color.

This recipe is very similar to traditional royal icing, but it does not contain glycerine. This makes it more appropriate for detailed piping work and gingerbread houses, when it needs to dry hard.

continued from previous page

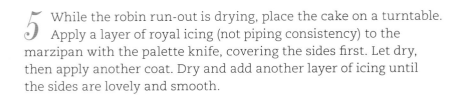

5 While the robin run-out is drying, place the cake on a turntable. Apply a layer of royal icing (not piping consistency) to the marzipan with the palette knife, covering the sides first. Let dry, then apply another coat. Dry and add another layer of icing until the sides are lovely and smooth.

6 When the sides are dry, frost the top, following the same steps. Try to get a sharp edge where the sides meet the top. Let dry. Place the cake on the royal-iced cake drum, taking care to center it. Fill 2 piping bags and attach a no. 1 tip to one bag and a no. 2 tip to the other. Pipe a row of dots onto the surface of the cake, where the top meets the sides. Create icicles by piping dots that become a little smaller as you work down the cake in vertical lines. Make the lines uneven in length, to provide a more realistic effect. When dry, dust with pearl luster dust.

7 Dust a flat surface with cornstarch, and roll out the red fondant to 1/16 in (2 mm) thick. Use the multi-ribbon cutter to cut a ribbon long enough to wrap around the base of the cake, 3/4 in (2 cm) wide. Moisten the back and wrap around the cake with the seam at the front. Roll out another length of red fondant and create a bow. Moisten the back and apply to the cake at the seam.

8 Very carefully lift the dry robin run-out from the acetate sheet, using a thin metal palette knife. You may have to move the knife gently from side to side to release it. Affix to the center of the cake with a small dot of royal icing. Dot a little royal icing onto the robin's wing portion of the run-out, and then carefully lift the second robin's wing on top, guiding it into place with your fingers. Allow to dry for about an hour.

9 Glue the satin ribbon around the base of the frosted cake drum, using craft glue. Pipe a few icicle dots over the seam at the back of the cake.

Tip

To create bauble mini cakes, form 2 in (5 cm) cake-pop balls (see p.242), and brush with jam. Wrap 4 1/2 oz (125 g) of fondant around each ball, smoothing, cutting off excess, and then rolling in your hands. Cover with festive fondant decorations.

Traditional fruitcake

This rich, dense cake is a popular choice for weddings and festivities. It also provides a strong base for stacked and layered cakes, and covers well with marzipan and royal icing, or fondant. Allow enough time to soak the fruit overnight at room temperature.

1 Simmer the first 7 ingredients in a large pot for 20 mins, until most liquid is absorbed. Remove from the heat. Let soak overnight.

2 Preheat the oven to 325°F (160°C). Beat the butter and sugar until fluffy. Mix in the eggs, one at a time.

4 Spoon the mixture into the pan; cover with foil. Bake for 2 hours. Uncover; bake for ½ hour, or until a skewer comes out clean. Let cool in the pan for 10 minutes, then turn onto a wire rack to cool completely. If desired, pour a tablespoon of brandy or whiskey over the cake.

3 Gently fold in the fruit mix and almonds. Sift over the rest of the dry ingredients and fold in, keeping the batter light and fluffy.

Ingredients

- 1⅓ cups golden raisins
- 1⅓ cups raisins
- 2½ cups prunes, chopped
- 2¼ cups candied cherries
- 2 small apples, peeled, cored, and diced
- 2 cups sweet cider
- 4 tsp pumpkin pie spice
- scant 1 cup unsalted butter, softened
- ¾ cup packed dark brown sugar
- 3 large eggs, lightly beaten
- 1⅓ cups ground almonds
- 2 cups all-purpose flour
- 2 tsp baking powder

Equipment

- 10in (25cm) deep, round springform cake pan, greased and lined

Marzipan

Marzipan is a thick, sweet almond paste that is traditionally used to cover fruitcakes underneath royal icing or fondant. It is also a great medium for modeling and even molding decorations for cakes. Its high sugar content allows it to last for months without refrigeration.

Ingredients

Makes 2 lb (900 g)

- ¾ cup granulated sugar
- 2½ cups confectioner's sugar, sifted, plus extra for rolling and kneading
- 4 cups ground almonds
- 1 tsp pure vanilla extract
- ½ tsp orange juice
- 2 large eggs, beaten

Tips

Marzipan can be colored in the same way as fondant. Knead a dab of coloring paste into the marzipan. Marzipan has a soft texture and will dry hard without a strengthener. Keep decorations in an airtight container once dry.

1 Mix both the sugars and ground almonds in a bowl. Make a well in the center and add the vanilla extract, orange juice, and eggs.

2 Use a palette knife to fold the wet ingredients gently into the dry ingredients, until you have a crumbly dough.

3 Dust a flat surface with confectioner's sugar, and knead the marzipan until smooth. Add more confectioner's sugar, if needed, to get the right consistency.

Piping royal icing runouts

Royal icing run-out, also known as "flood work," involves piping royal icing into a shape and allowing it to dry until hard. You can use the decoration as part of a 3-D cake topping, or lay it flat to embellish cakes, cookies, gingerbread, and cupcakes. Be careful, since it will be fragile.

1 Lay the acetate sheet on the template so that the template is visible. Lightly grease the acetate with vegetable shortening. You can also lay the template on top of a piece of parchment paper and trace the shape, if preferred.

2 Using the small, fine tip, pipe royal icing around the outline of the shape. Allow to dry for a couple of hours to create a "dam." If you are using different colors on the surface, pipe in outlines now, and let everything dry.

3 Spritz the royal icing with water, or add it drop by drop until the icing is roughly the consistency of shampoo. Draw a spoon through the surface. If the line created fills in 10 seconds, it is redy for flooding. Fill a piping bag attached to the large tip, with the thin royal icing. Press down on the piping bag and "flood" the template with icing, working from the center outward until the entire surface of the design is covered. Gently tap the board or surface beneath the shape to release any air bubbles.

4 Allow to dry for 24 hours before applying details. Lift the decoration away from the acetate sheet with a palette knife and carefully apply to the cake with a dab of royal icing. Alternatively, you could attach to a cake-pop stick or wire with a dab of royal icing.

Ingredients

- vegetable shortening, for greasing
- royal icing), tinted or colored, as desired

Equipment

- food-grade acetate sheets
- cardboard or parchment paper template
- piping bags with small, fine, circular piping tip and large circular piping tip

Runout robin

Wing

NOTE
photocopy at 100%

Prepare Christmas drinks

Winter is the time to enjoy warming drinks to keep the chilly weather at bay, so if you want to serve something other than Champagne or wine, try these fruity seasonal drinks. The Old-fashioned rum with a twist takes a little more time and care to prepare than the others, but it's worth the effort.

Old-fashioned rum with a twist

Put the honey and 1 tablespoon of rum in a Rocks glass. Stir the mixture until the honey has mixed into the rum. Add 1 ice cube and 1 mint leaf and stir until the ice has nearly melted. Add another tablespoon of rum and another ice cube. Stir until the ice cube has partly melted. Add the rest of the rum and one more ice cube. Stir the drink 15 times or so and then fill the glass to the top with ice cubes. Take a piece of pared lime rind, crack it over the glass to release the oils from the skin, and serve.

Ingredients

For each drink:

- 2 tbsp sugar syrup
- 2fl oz (50 ml) aged rum
- Ice cubes
- 1 fresh mint leaf
- Pared lime rind, to garnish

Spiced fruit cocktail

Peel and slice the pear and place it in the bottom of a cocktail shaker. Add the plum jam and ground cinnamon and muddle down (a muddler is a barman's wooden utensil used to crush hard ingredients to release flavors; the handle of a wooden spoon can be used instead). Add the Cognac, apple juice, and some ice. Shake and strain the mixture into a cocktail glass, add a few drops of lemon juice, and serve.

For each drink:

- 1 pear
- 1 tsp plum jam
- 1 pinch ground cinnamon
- 2fl oz (50 ml) Cognac
- 2fl oz (50 ml) apple juice
- Ice cubes
- A few drops of fresh lemon juice

Fruit fizz

Put some ice cubes into a tall tumbler or highball glass. Pour in equal amounts of the orange and cranberry juice, and the lemonade. Stir well and serve.

For each drink:

- Ice cubes
- ⅓ glass fresh orange juice, chilled
- ⅓ glass cranberry juice, chilled
- ⅓ glass organic lemonade, chilled

Make flavored alcohol

If you gather blackberries from hedgerows in the fall, or if you have a bountiful harvest of raspberries or other fruits, turn some of the crop into fruity flavored alcoholic drinks. Use gin or vodka with the highest proof content to get the best preserving results. These wonderfully warming drinks take three and a half months to mature, and then continue to improve in flavor.

Alcohol is a preservative—nothing can grow in pure alcohol—and when fruits are soaked in it, the alcohol absorbs their flavor to give a fruity taste and color. Use ripe produce for the best quality and flavor and freeze the fruits until needed. Frozen fruit provides excellent results: the freezing process ruptures the fruit skins and allows the juices to flow out.

To make Raspberry gin

Ingredients

To make about 1 quart (c. 1 liter):

- 1 bottle of gin (1¼ pints/700 ml)
- 2 cups raspberries, fresh or frozen
- 1 cup superfine sugar
- A few cloves (optional)
- 1 stick of cinnamon (optional)
- A few drops of almond extract (optional)
- 1 large, wide-necked jar, sterilized, or 2 empty gin bottles

Pour the gin, fruit, sugar, spices, and almond extract into the sterilized jar, or divide the ingredients equally between two bottles using a funnel (there's no need to sterilize a vodka or gin bottle if the alcohol has just been poured out of it). Seal and store in a cool, dark place. Give the jar or bottles a shake daily for the first two weeks and then weekly for a further three months. During this time the sugar dissolves and the liquor takes on a luscious red color. Take a sip every now and then and add more sugar if needed. After three and half months, or when the taste is to your liking, strain the ingredients, and re-bottle the liquid only.

Variation To make Sloe gin, replace the raspberries with sloes and prick each sloe berry with a skewer before adding to the gin. To make Blackberry or Damson (Italian plum) vodka, replace the gin with vodka and the raspberries with blackberries or damsons.

Use a muslin bag to strain the alcohol and fruits. Suspend the muslin with two bamboo sticks and collect the alcohol in a bowl.

Make mulled drinks

Winter is the time to enjoy warming drinks to keep the chilly weather at bay. Mulled drinks have long been part of our winter traditions: mead—a fermented drink made of honey, water, and yeast—was flavored with spices and sometimes fruits, and heated by plunging a hot poker into the liquid; and wassail, a hot, spiced punch often associated with winter celebrations in northern Europe, derives from medieval times, when it was more like a mulled beer seasoned with spices and honey. These drinks are easy to prepare and taste delicious.

Mulled wine can be left warming on the stove all evening, but don't let it boil or the alcohol will evaporate. If you want to prepare it ahead of time, heat the wine, spices, lemon rind, sugar, and the orange studded with cloves to simmering point, turn off the heat, and leave to marinate for a few hours before adding the orange juice, brandy, and orange slices.

Mulled wine

Pour 2 bottles of red wine into a large pan and add 1 orange studded with 12 cloves, the pared zest of 1 lemon, a 2 in (5 cm) piece of fresh ginger, peeled and cut into slices, 2 cinnamon sticks, 4 tablespoons of brandy, $^1\!/_2$ cup demerara sugar, the juice of 1 orange, and 1 thinly sliced orange. Bring almost to the boil on a medium heat, stirring until the sugar has dissolved. Turn the heat down and simmer for 30 minutes, then serve in glasses.

Hot pear cup

Cut $^1\!/_2$ a crisp apple into slices and stud each slice with a couple of cloves. Place the slices in a large pan, add $3^1\!/_2$ cups pear cider, 1 vanilla bean, 1 large piece of pared lemon zest, $^2\!/_3$ cup brandy, 1 cinnamon stick, 2 tablespoons of honey, and bring to the boil. Simmer gently for 10 minutes, then serve in four glasses.

Winter whiskey sour

Stud 4 lemon slices with 3 cloves each. Place in a pan with 1 strip of lemon rind, 2 tablespoons of maple syrup, and $1^3\!/_4$ cups water. Bring to the boil, then turn off the heat and leave to infuse for 5 minutes. Divide a $^1\!/_2$ cup whiskey and the 4 lemon slices between 4 glasses, discard the lemon rind, add the infused water, and serve.

Mulled-wine kit

Red wine that has been heated, or mulled and flavored is a well-loved Christmas drink, and a mulled-wine kit is the perfect present for someone who enjoys its warming, spicy undertones. When you tie the spice sachet to the bottle, add a gift label with instructions for making the mulled wine and what other ingredients to add. One kit should be enough for about six glasses.

1 Prepare the spices: break the cinnamon stick into three pieces, crush the cardamom pods lightly, and grate a little fresh nutmeg.

2 Place the cinnamon, cardamom, nutmeg, and cloves in the center of the cheesecloth square. Measure out the ginger and add it to the spices.

3 Gather the four corners of the cheesecloth and hold them with the fingertips of one hand. Gather up the four remaining corners.

4 Wrap the piece of twine around the top of the sachet and secure it tightly. Then tie the loose ends of the twine around the neck of the bottle.

Ingredients

- 1 cinnamon stick
- 6 cardamom pods, lightly crushed
- Fresh nutmeg
- 12 cloves
- 1 pinch ground ginger
- 1 bottle red wine

Equipment

- 1 square cheesecloth, about 7 x 7 in (18 x 18 cm)
- A length of twine

Mulled wine instructions
Put the wine, sachet, half a cup of water, and 6 tablespoons granulated or demerara sugar into a pan. Heat gently until the sugar has dissolved, but do not boil. Ingredients to add: a splash of brandy, gin, Cointreau, port, or the juice of 1 orange.

Templates

4

Fabric garland

See pages 16–19. Make templates of the shapes that you like and cut out two of each shape, except for the robin's body and beak, for which you should cut out one of each shape, and the holly leaf, for which you should cut out four shapes.

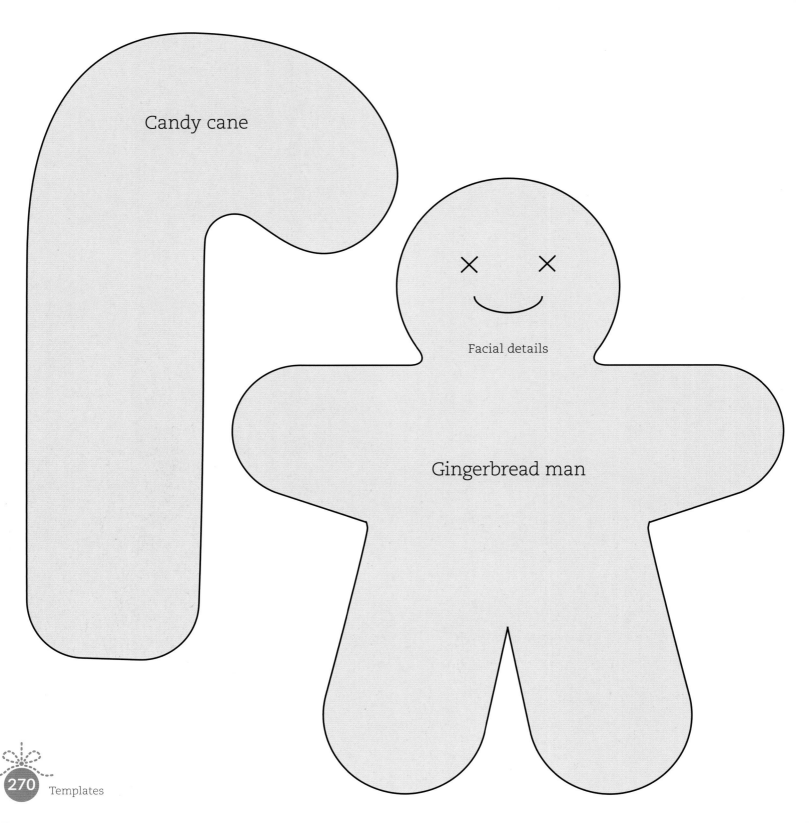

Candy cane

Facial details

Gingerbread man

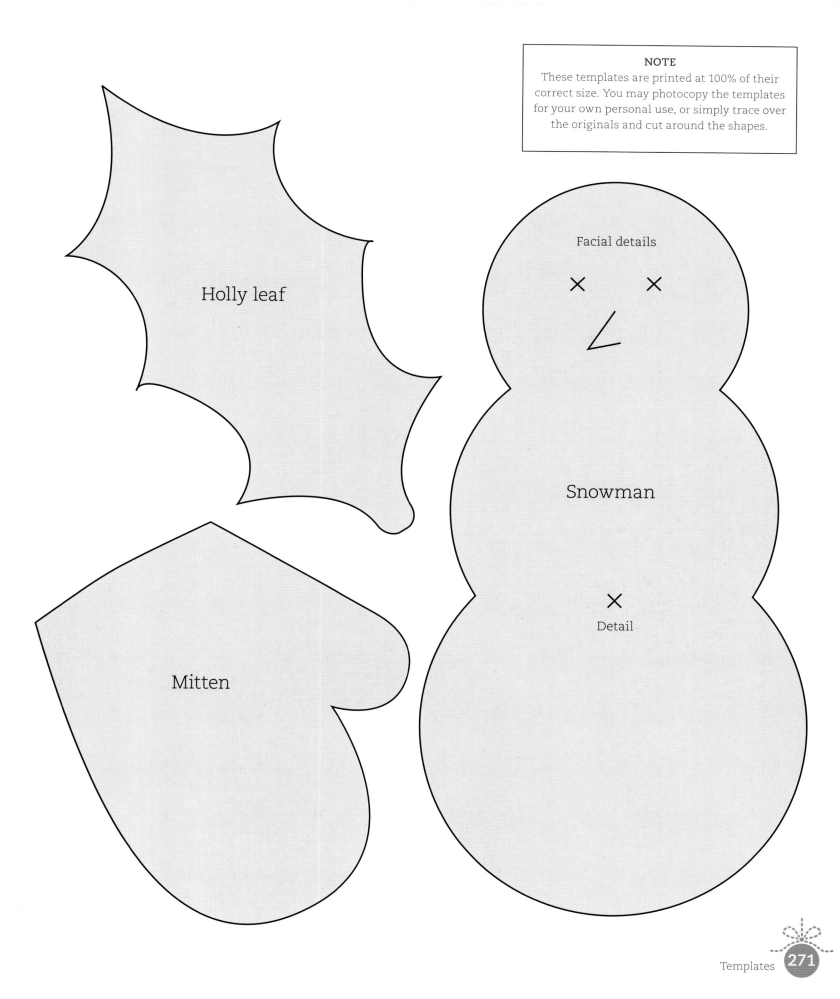

Holly leaf

Facial details

Snowman

Detail

Mitten

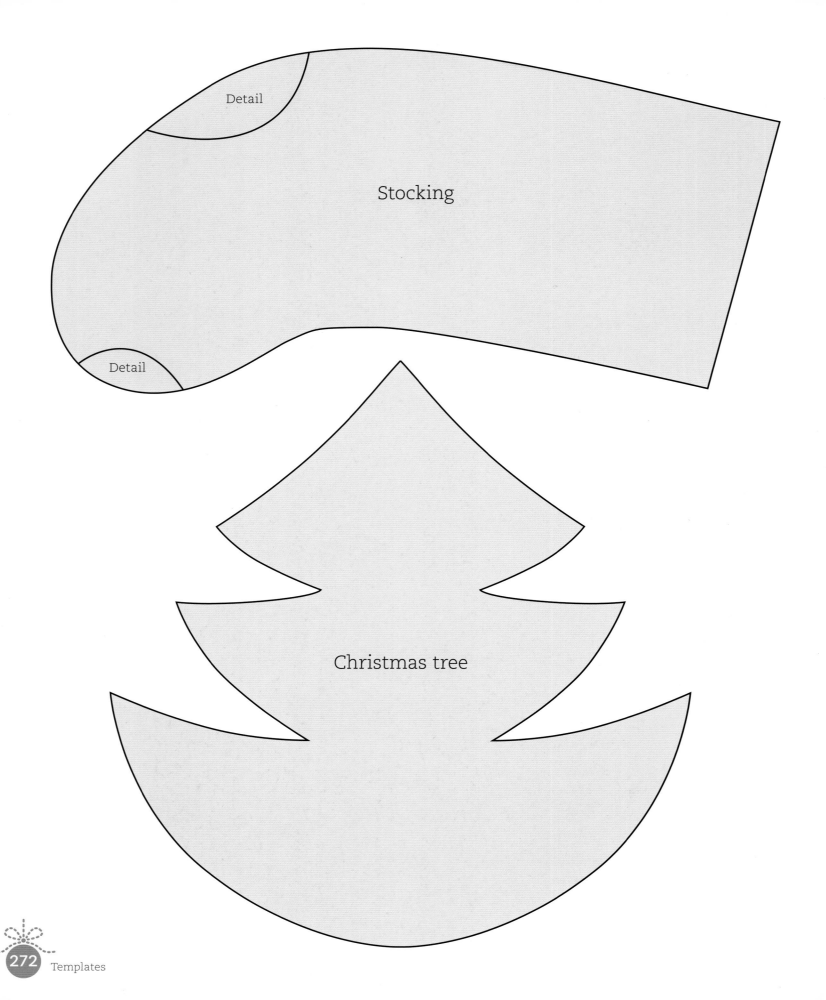

Stocking

Detail

Detail

Christmas tree

NOTE

These templates are printed at 100% of their correct size. You may photocopy the templates for your own personal use, or simply trace over the originals and cut around the shapes.

Robin's breast

Robin's wing

Fold

Robin's beak

Robin's body

Christmas stocking

See pages 20–21. For each stocking, cut out two shapes from the template.

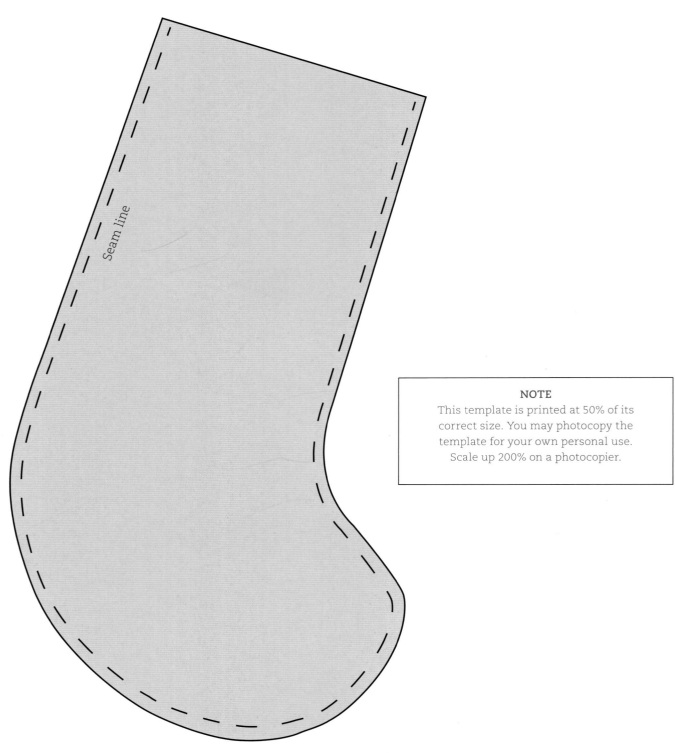

Seam line

NOTE
This template is printed at 50% of its
correct size. You may photocopy the
template for your own personal use.
Scale up 200% on a photocopier.

Doll pin tree angel

See pages 58–59. Make up the templates and cut out two angel dress shapes in fabric and one wing shape in felt.

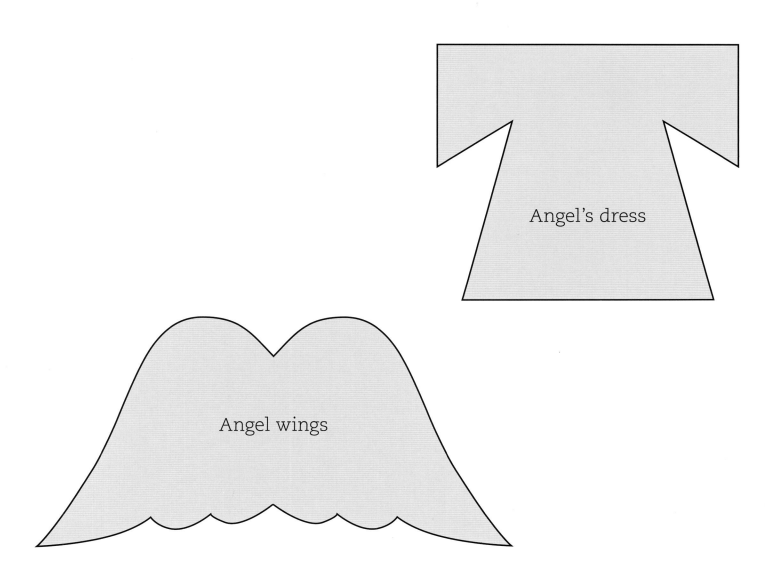

Angel's dress

Angel wings

NOTE
This template is printed at 50% of its correct size. You may photocopy the template for your own personal use. Scale up 200% on a photocopier.

Festive birds

See pages 46–47. For each bird, make up the templates and cut out two body shapes, two wing shapes, and several flowers and leaves.

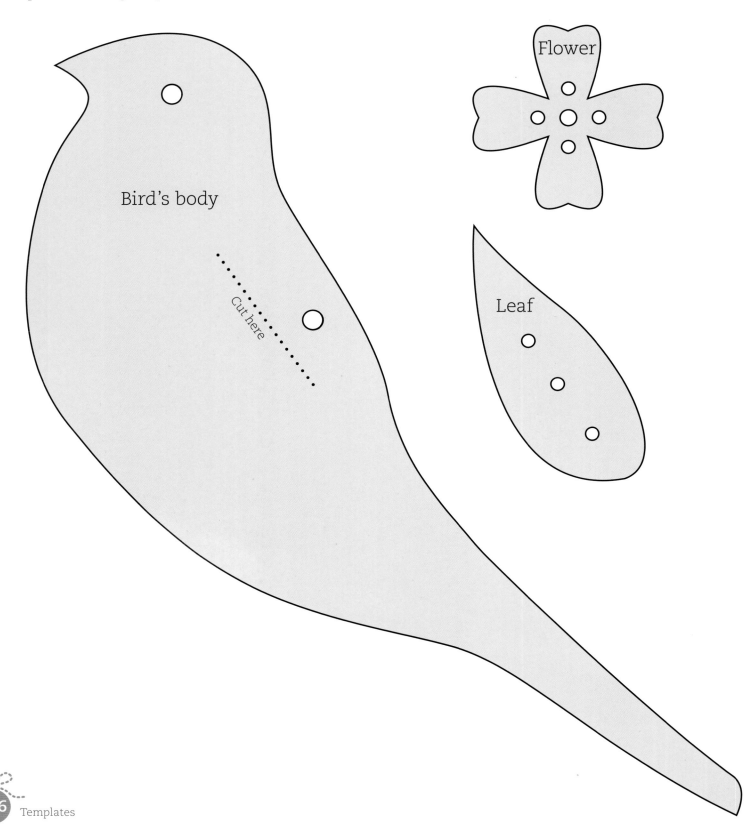

Flower

Bird's body

Cut here

Leaf

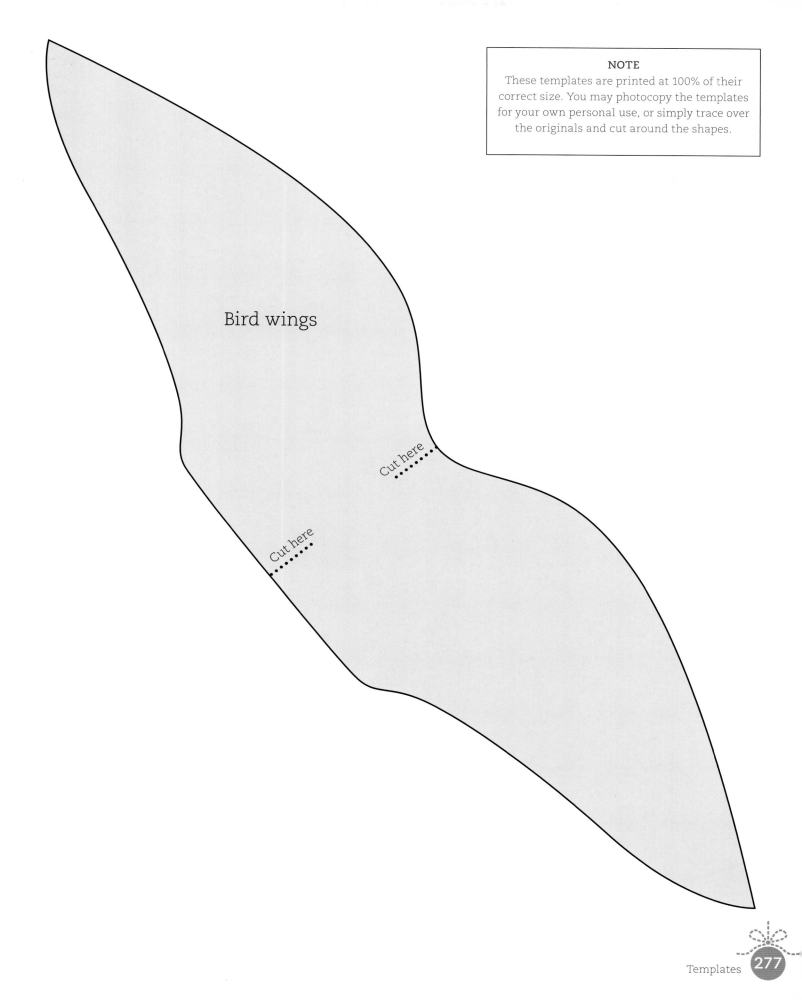

Bird wings

Cut here

Cut here

Paper and fabric cards and decorations

See pages 50–51, 150–51, and 154–55.

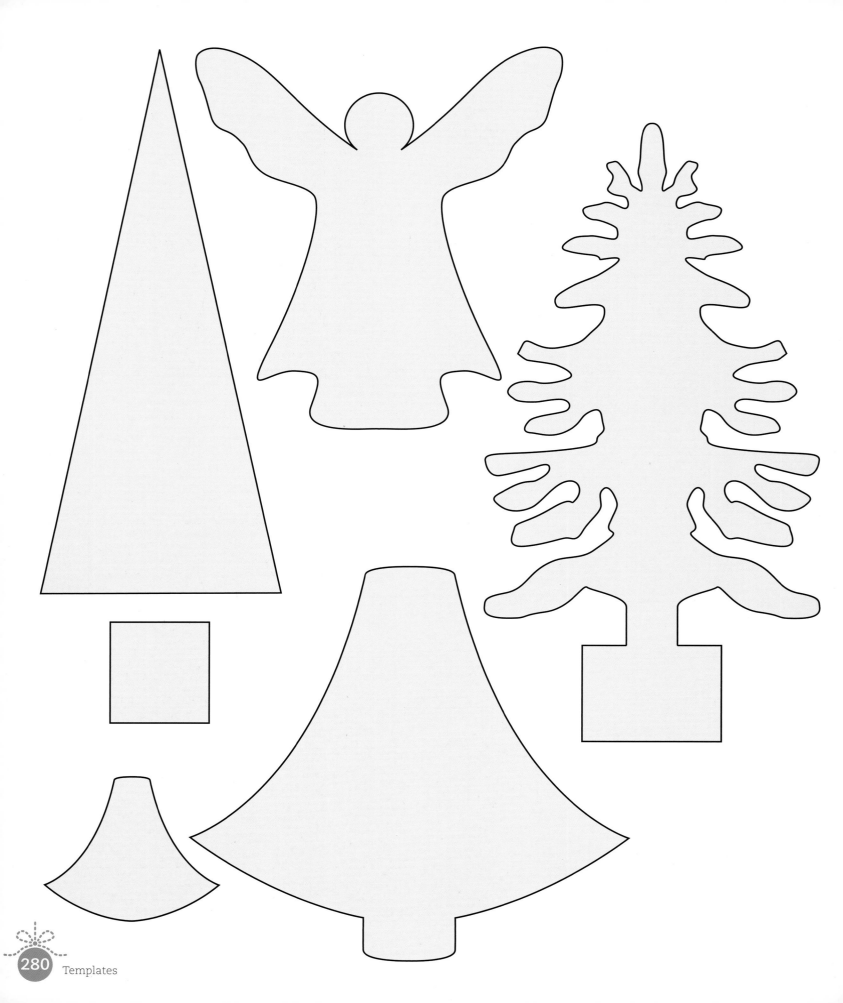

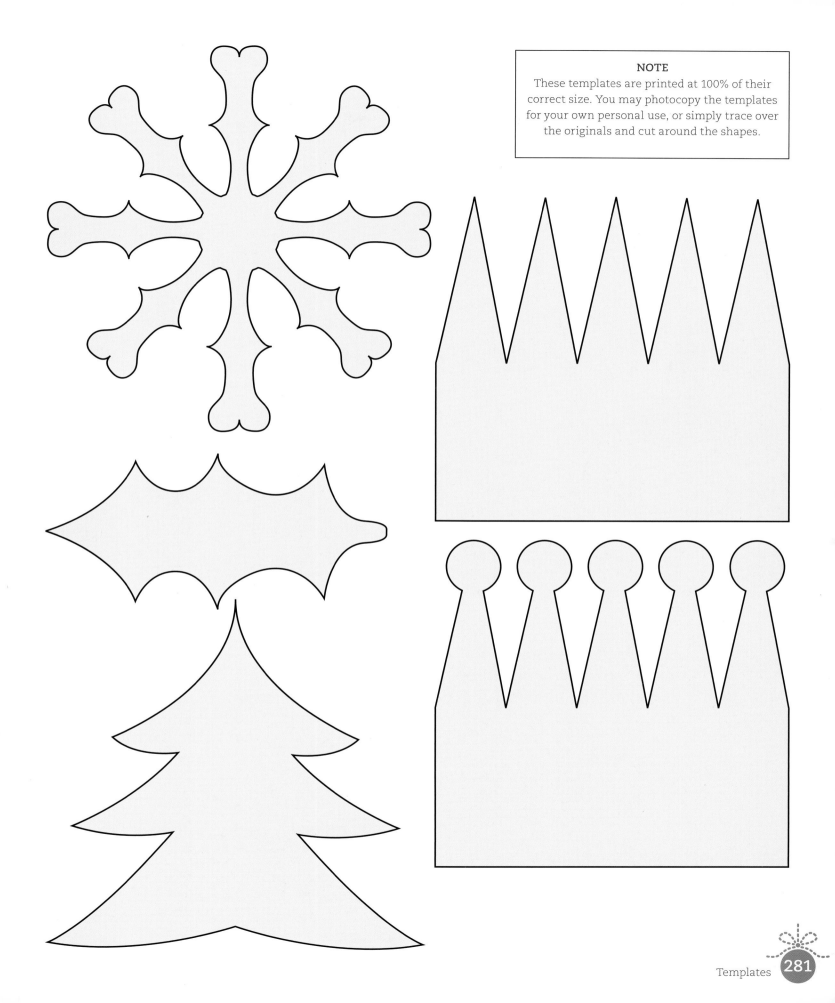

Scented fabric hearts

See pages 52–53. For each fabric heart, cut two shapes from the template.

Seam line

NOTE
These templates are printed at 100% of their correct size. You may photocopy the templates for your own personal use, or simply trace over the originals and cut around the shapes.

Candy cane cones

See pages 56–57. For each cone, cut out one felt shape and one fabric shape from the template.

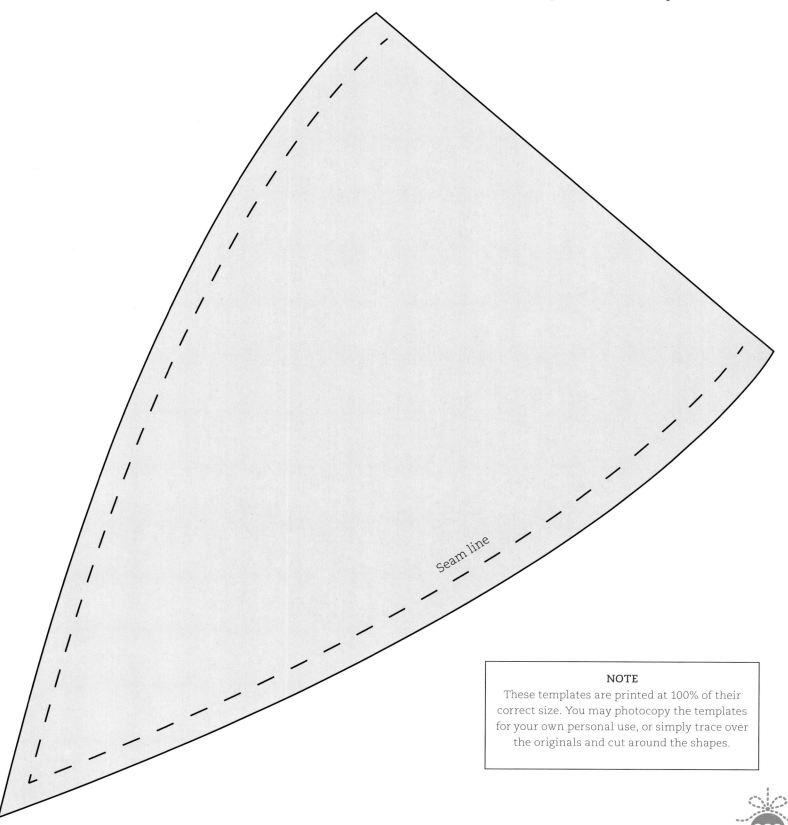

Seam line

NOTE

These templates are printed at 100% of their correct size. You may photocopy the templates for your own personal use, or simply trace over the originals and cut around the shapes.

Advent calendar sacks

See pages 54–55. For each sack, cut out two shapes from the template.

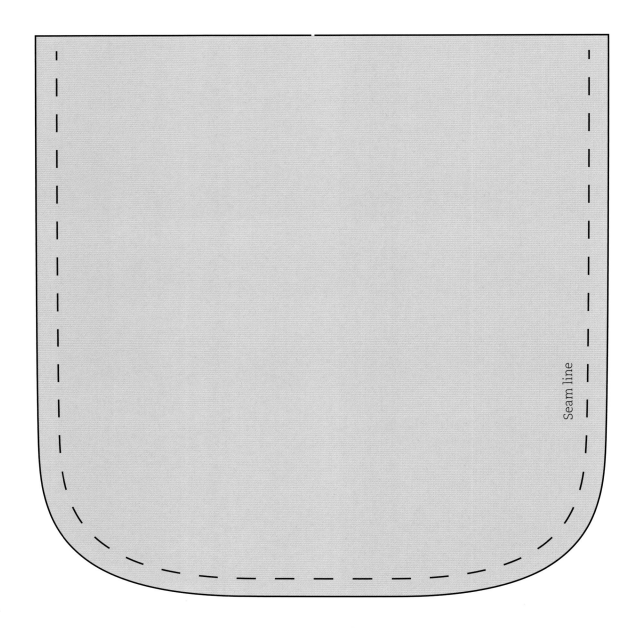

Seam line

NOTE

These templates are printed at 100% of their correct size. You may photocopy the templates for your own personal use, or simply trace over the originals and cut around the shapes.

Silver clay jewelry

See pages 68–69.

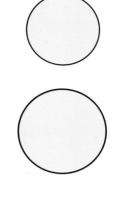

Wallpaper
earrings
template

Leaf
template

Heart keyring
template

Button
cufflink
templates

NOTE

These templates are printed at 100% of their
correct size. You may photocopy the templates
for your own personal use, or simply trace over
the originals and cut around the shapes.

Hot-water bottle cover

See pages 140–41. For each hot-water bottle cover, cut out one shape from the front
cover template, and one shape from each of the back cover templates. Cut out two
shapes from either the heart or star template.

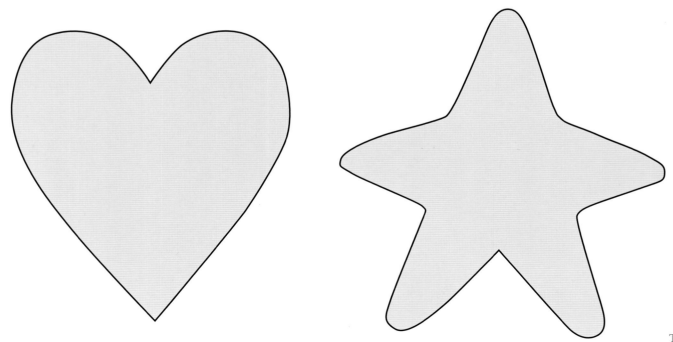

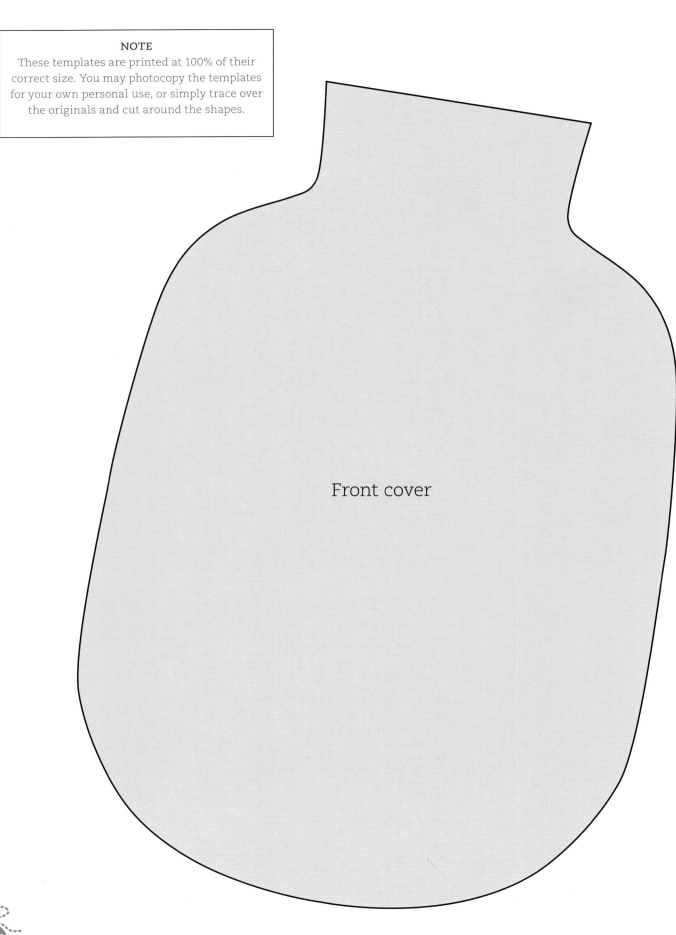

Front cover

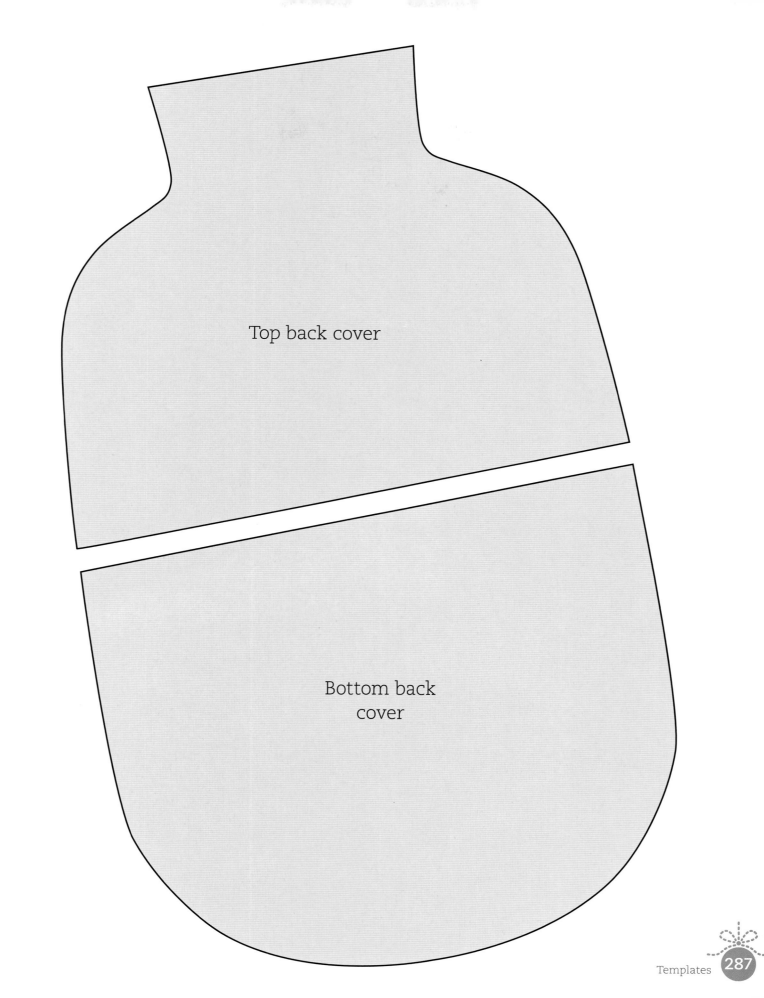

Top back cover

Bottom back
cover

Gingerbread house

Scan and use these panels to cut out gingerbread pieces to build your Gingerbread house (see p.248).

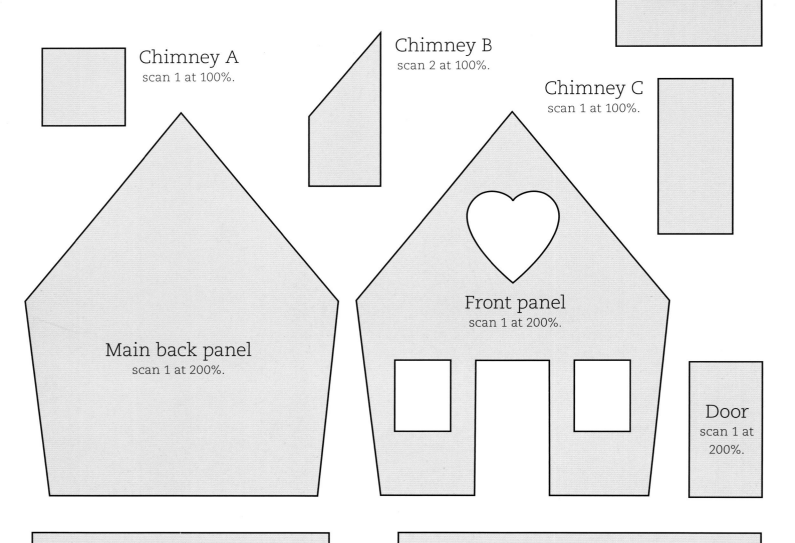

Chimney D
scan 1 at 100%.

Chimney A
scan 1 at 100%.

Chimney B
scan 2 at 100%.

Chimney C
scan 1 at 100%.

Main back panel
scan 1 at 200%.

Front panel
scan 1 at 200%.

Door
scan 1 at 200%.

Wall panels
scan 2 at 200%.

Roof panel
scan 2 at 200%.

Square gift box template

This template makes the box on pp.156–57.
Please enlarge to the required
size on a photocopier.

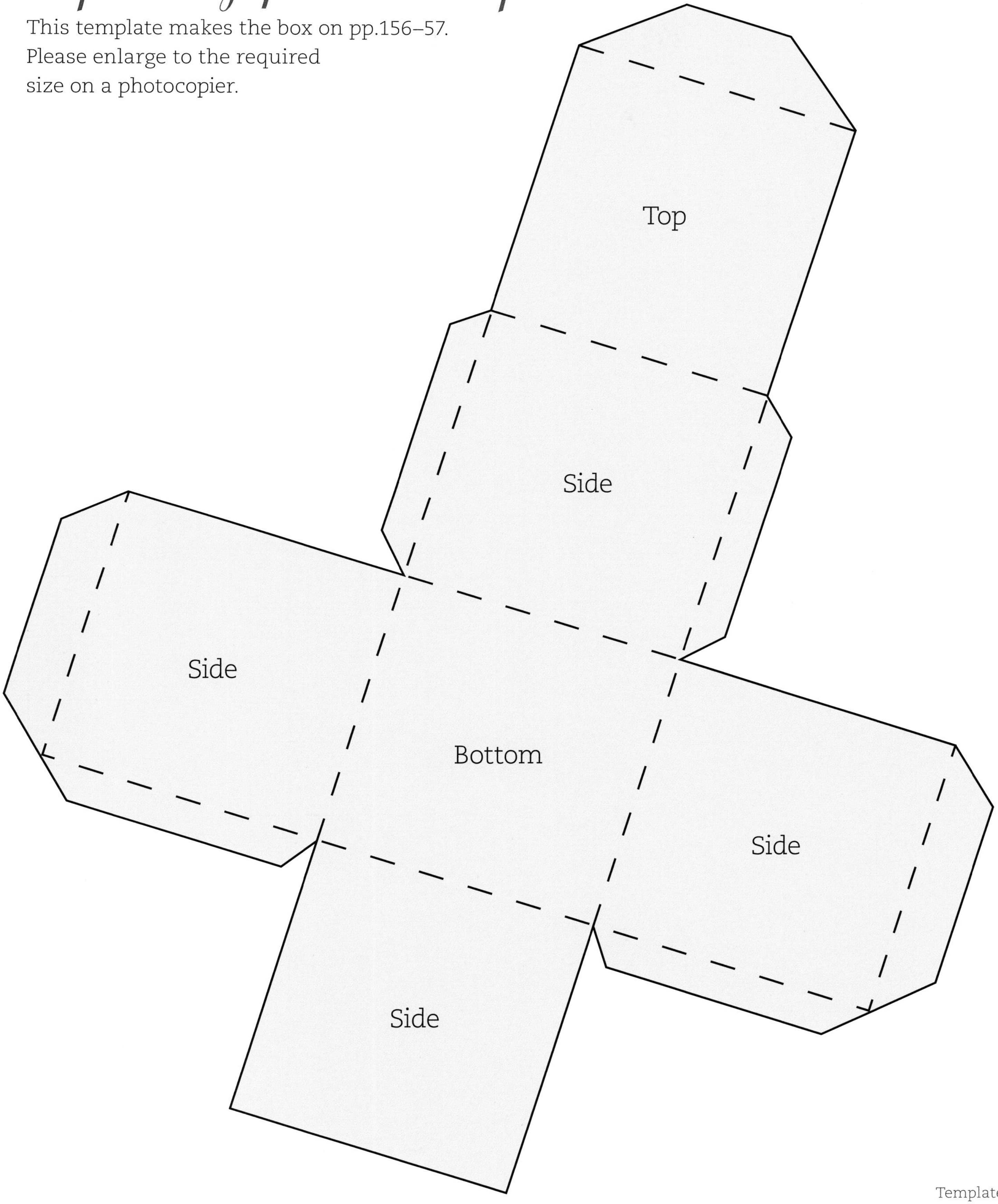

Top

Side

Side

Bottom

Side

Side

Side

Jewelery case template

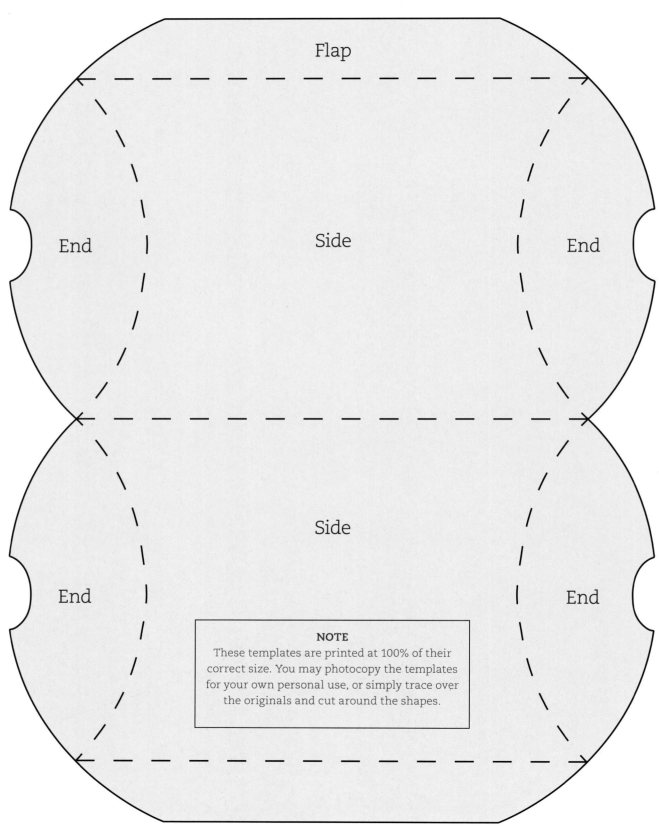

Flap

End

Side

End

End

Side

End

NOTE
These templates are printed at 100% of their correct size. You may photocopy the templates for your own personal use, or simply trace over the originals and cut around the shapes.

Pyramid box template

Please enlarge to the required size on a photocopier

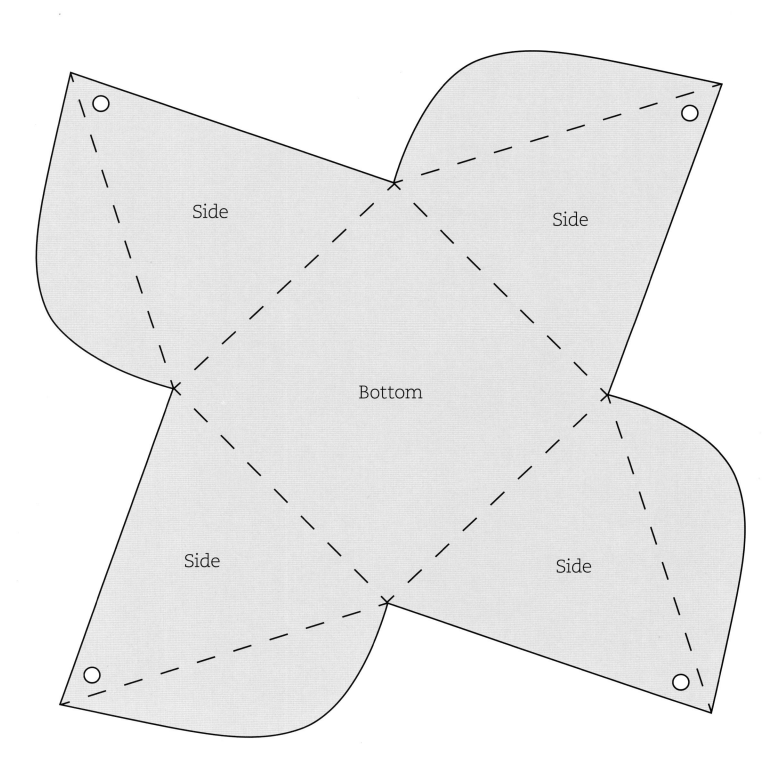

Side

Side

Bottom

Side

Side

Index

Acknowledgments

Sheherazade Goldsmith would like to thank: Susannah Steel for writing the book and agreeing with all my ideas and edits. Jo Fairley for her workable beauty recipes. Ted & Harry for the prettiest recycled fabric decorations I have ever seen, and all the crafts people; Barbara Coupe, Francine Raymond, Lucy Harrington, Made in Hastings, Sparrowkids, Isabel de Cordova and Caroline Zoob. Richard Scott for his delicious recipes and Kirsty Trotter for her endless patience. Peter Anderson for his beautiful photographs and everyone at DK. Lastly, my kids for making Christmas so much fun.

DK would like to thank all the crafters who created the projects that appear in this book, Valerie Lane-Glover and Pammie Riggs for valuable advice, Mike Wells, Jane at Not Just Food Ltd for testing the recipes, and Vanessa Bird and Constance Novis for the index.